ROSIE'S S

7/16/06

ROSIE'S SECRET PASSION

RESTORING THE ANCIENT FAITH OF
OUR MOTHERS

To Betty,

May the Lord bless you to keep growing & seeking & sharing your love with others,

Akila T. Karanja

TRUE VINE PUBLISHING

South Bend, Indiana

Love,

Akila Karanja

Copyright 2002 by Akila T. Karanja

True Vine Publishing

P.O. Box 1614, South Bend, IN 46634, USA

akilakaranja@yahoo.com

Editor, Elizabeth Watson, PhD

Cover Design, Akila T. Karanja

PRINTED IN U.S.A

ISBN: 0-9745541-0-3

DEDICATION

T his book is dedicated to my mother, Melverine, who told me I can do anything I put my mind to.
I love you, Mama.

To my grandmothers; Elizabeth and Melba, my great aunt Charity and all my foremothers, I pray that your faith may be rewarded and clothed with eternal life.

To Dell-Amina, Yejide and Wambui, my beautiful daughters, I love you, too. I pray that you learn your lessons well and obtain the mastery over your circumstances.

To struggling and neglected and beautiful women everywhere. Your blessing is on its way.

ACKNOWLEDGMENTS

I acknowledge my husband, Joseph, for love and acceptance, our children, Njaaga, Dell-Amina, Yejide, Kambai and Wambui for giving me "tough skin," Juliette for inspiration and friendship, Vibiana (Koko) for heralding my future in Christ, Elizabeth for believing in me, and Dr. Watson for editing this book and validating me as an author.

I acknowledge all of my relatives, brothers, sisters, cousins, uncles, aunties and friends with special thanks to my father, Eugene for the tip on book proposals, Eleanore, my step father, James, Aunt Mavis and Uncle Count. You are my family and I love you.

I acknowledge my extended family, including Rasheedah, Loretha and Frank. I am grateful for my friends who are in the many congregations to which I have belonged. Thank you for being my mothers, fathers, sisters, brothers and friends. I look forward to spending an eternity with you under the watchful eye of God Almighty.

FOREWORD

One day while cleaning up I looked in the kitchen garbage can, and something at the top of the full rubbish pile caught my attention. It was my niece's baby doll. The doll was fully undressed and its disheveled hair shot up in all directions. Its pretty brown eyes were open, some of the eyelashes missing. The head of the doll was hanging off of the body, and the fiber filling could be seen clearly coming out of the doll's neck because of threads which had become loosened. This doll was in sad shape.

I could not bear to leave Nakiah's doll in the garbage can. It reminded me of myself, a real little girl whom my grandfather decided would serve to relieve him of his sexual passion. It reminded me of Mary Magdalene, a real woman whom some men attempted to discard as useless at the feet of Jesus.

I picked Nakiah's doll up and out of the rubbish. Surely she did not deserve to be discarded as useless. I sewed the head back onto the neck of the body; it was a simple and successful operation. I covered the doll with a white cloth, head and body, and I called her Mary. I then displayed her in a very prominent place.

We often find mangled lives in trash piles, discarded as refuse. Fortunately, the breath of life remains in some of us. This book is dedicated to the resurrection of the multitudes of Marys and Rosies who lie in the many rubbish heaps of life. May we all be blessed. May we all be lifted by the hands of Jesus, our accusers fleeing.

ATK

CONTENTS

ISAIAH 58:6-12

"Is not this the fast that I have chosen? to loose the bands of wickedness, to undo the heavy burdens, and to let the oppressed go free, and that ye break every yoke? Is it not to deal thy bread to the hungry, and that thou bring the poor that are cast out to thy house? when thou seest the naked, that thou cover him; and that thou hide not thyself from thine own flesh?

"Then shall thy light break forth as the morning, and thine health shall spring forth speedily: and thy righteousness shall go before thee; the glory of the Lord shall be thy rereward. Then shalt thou call, and the Lord shall answer; thou shalt cry and he shall say, Here I am.

"If thou take away from the midst of thee the yoke, the putting forth of the finger, and speaking vanity; And if thou draw out thy soul to the hungry, and satisfy the afflicted soul; then shall thy light rise in obscurity, and thy darkness be as the noon day: And the Lord shall guide thee continually, and satisfy thy soul in drought, and make fat thy bones; and thou shalt be like a watered garden, and like a spring of water, whose waters fail not.

"And they that shall be of thee shall build the old waste places: thou shalt raise up the foundations of many generations; and thou shalt be called, The repairer of the breach, The restorer of paths to dwell in."

ROSIE'S SECRET PASSION

RESTORING THE ANCIENT FAITH OF OUR MOTHERS

O**ne**

THE ABORTION

T he weather was neither sweet nor dismal. It was just a normal day. Rosie walked into the clinic and Bigmama followed close behind her. Guilt pushed the young woman forward with the intensity of the steel nose of a gun poking her in the back. There was not a smile between the two. They just walked in and sat down. There was business that needed to be taken care of, and it was urgent.

Rosie wanted to run, but she was stayed by her grandmother's arguments that she was in no position to raise a child out of wedlock and that the best thing to do was to abort the baby. Rosie wanted to stand up and tell everybody in the clinic to run for their babies' lives, but she was stayed by cowardice and guilt and shame. The joy that she felt in her secret place with the new life that grew in her womb was turned into depression and remorse when somehow the secret got out to her grandmother that she was pregnant.

"Rosie Brown," called the receptionist as she opened the sliding glass window. "It's my turn," said Rosie to herself. She looked deeply into the eyes of the many other women in the room. Only God knew why they were here. She clung with all of her might to the hope that she could save all of the babies, but not a sound of protest came from her mouth. She just followed the nurse, uneasily, yet compliantly.

It was quick. It was easy. It was virtually painless. Then the nurse gave Rosie grape juice and graham crackers. Shortly thereafter, she was released to go. When they left the clinic, Bigmama and Rosie, the sun was shining brightly. But Rosie could hardly see. Her future was still a mystery. The child that had been growing inside of her, making her sick to the stomach, was now gone.

T^{wo}

A GENERATION OF CURSES

Rosie's grandmother was raised in the South in the 20's and 30's. Rosie called her Bigmama. Bigmama was a pretty woman, and she put much stock in her beauty. She married a man from her home community, and soon thereafter he joined the United States Army. He would not allow her to live in the army barracks with him.

After some time she decided she would move to California. Against the wishes of her husband that she leave their baby in Arkansas with his parents, she took her 2-year-old daughter with her to Califorina. Bigmama then became the wife of a man who had migrated to California from

Louisiana. He, too, put much stock in his looks. He was a tall, fair-skinned black man who had wavy hair. By many accounts, he was a joy to behold.

There was much ado in "small town" Arkansas about Rosie's grandmother marrying the man from Louisiana. The way Rosie's great grandmother put it, the people were hard on her Bigmama, saying she left her husband for another man. Rosie's great grandmother said that Bigmama's first husband had another woman, too. The women in Rosie's family usually stuck together and kept their mouths shut in unison about things that were painfully embarrassing even if they were morally wrong. Eventually, the secret oozed out like a sticky mess.

Bigmama took great pains to show forth a face of dignity in the wake of her broken home. By the time that Rosie was born, however, her grandmother frowned and worried and groaned in pain from the effects of high blood pressure, mini heart attacks, her troubles and troubles in the lives of her relatives.

Rosie loved her grandmother. She smelled like ice cream and candy and sometimes she smelled like Este Lauder perfume. She was soft and smooth and gentle. She listened to Rosie, and she gave her hope. She spoke to Rosie often about strength and infallibility. She said, "Keep your hand in the hand of the man upstairs." Bigmama was talking about God's hand. Bigmama was generous. When she cooked, she cooked a lot of food, enough for the people in her house to eat and enough for the guests who might come, too.

One day Rosie was at her grandparents' house while her grandfather was on his way to work. He was a security guard, but he looked like a policeman. He had a full uniform, a badge, a hat and a gun in his holster on his side. Bigmama had fried some chicken. Rosie could smell it in the house everywhere she went, and she could hardly wait to eat it.

Rosie's grandfather, Bigdaddy also liked fried chicken, and as he prepared his lunch for work he took all of the choice pieces of the meat on the stove. Rosie was standing in the kitchen while he was doing it, and her heart sank with disappointment. But Bigmama beckoned Rosie with her eyes and a slight smile. She was encouraging Rosie not to lose heart. When Bigdaddy turned around, Bigmama opened the cabinet door where the plates were kept to display a plate full of golden brown, fried chicken legs. Then Bigmama smiled broadly at Rosie. Rosie smiled gratefully at her grandmother and she gave her grandfather a warm goodbye. When Bigdaddy left, Rosie and Bigmama ate chicken until they were satisfied.

Rosie loved her grandfather, too, her grandmother's second husband. Although Bigdaddy was Rosie's step-grandfather, she did not know it for a long while. When she did find out his true familial relationship to her, it did not change how she related to him. She figured she had nothing to do with her grandfather's relationship to her grandmother. Bigdaddy smelled like bourbon and whiskey, butterscotch candy and Bruit cologne. He liked to laugh and joke around. He liked talking about people. Gossip was commonplace in Bigmama's house.

Sometimes Bigdaddy would lift Rosie up to the old-fashioned light fixture which dangled from the kitchen ceiling. She would reach her little hand up to yank the chain down and turn the light on and off. That was one of Rosie's favorite pastimes. Rosie felt so special when she was in her grandfather's arms.

Bigdaddy would often ask Rosie,

"When I kick off and go to heaven, what you gon' do"?

Rosie would reply by saying,

"I'm going with you."

Bigdaddy would whistle quietly at Rosie sometimes and wink his eye and give her a sip of the alcohol in his glass. Bigmama gave Rosie alcohol sometimes, too.

Bigdaddy and Bigmama argued much of the time they spent in Rosie's presence. It appeared as though they did not agree on many things. He would state his case and smile and laugh confidently about his rightness. She would make her case bitterly and frown about her rightness.

They would sit in the same chairs most of the time. Bigmama's chair was by the two windows and by the huge house plant which grew so tall that it bent at the ceiling. Bigdaddy had two chairs. One of them was beneath the painting of the peaceful country scene which hung on the livingroom wall. The other chair was a recliner, and it sat near the kitchen. The television set was near the front door. Sometimes Bigmama and Bigdaddy argued and watched TV and read the newspaper all at the same time. Sometimes they just watched TV and read the newspaper.

Bigmama had very definite opinions about what she read and heard in the news about the drug culture. She read about the violence of the violent and about the wickedness of the wicked and what should happen to the drug dealers and their clan. She believed they should be brought to justice and be stopped from hurting even one of her little ones. But in the face of her opinions about others, she had little power to reverse the downward spiral of her own life.

Bigmama, like the drug dealers, sought to hide from authority, the authority of the face she saw in the mirror, that which pointed out her iniquity, that face which sought her conviction that she, too, might be brought to justice. Rosie saw through her grandmother's facade to what laid just beneath the surface.

It came to pass that Bigmama became wearied by the physical, emotional and psychological abuse she suffered at the hand of her husband. Rosie's grandfather repeatedly beat his wife and threatened her with impending doom as he loaded his pistol and pointed it directly at her, daring her to call the police. She would never call the police, and she refused to leave him.

In order to mask her pain, she contracted with the

drug dealer. She said she needed "to calm her nerves." Though the penalty she wished against the drug dealer was stiff, she acknowledged the benefit of his service. Her drug of choice was perfectly legal, though.

She did not go to the inner city highways and byways to contract with the underworld lords. But she did choose to numb her pain rather than eradicate it.

Her doctor wrote her a prescription for legal medicine which was filled by the pharmacist. As she took her "pills" she hid her face from the one who looked at her from the mirror of her mind. The only one who could remove the facade that masqueraded itself as herself was effectively quieted as she reconciled herself to live the life she was too fearful to change.

Because of the many reasons Bigmama must have told herself she had for continuing to live with her second husband, she not only suffered abuse, but she subjected her children to the pain of abuse as well.

Rosie's grandfather was a wolf in sheep's clothing. His desire was unto himself, and it was unholy. He would sing religious songs and go to church and drink bourbon and beer and play poker and gamble and beat his wife and wear nice clothes and molest his daughter and hypnotize the people as he became the life of the party at family functions, and he molested Rosie.

The passion of this man, his anger, his sex life and his victims were all rolled up into one. He was an enemy in his house instead of a fit head of his family. Surely if it were revealed the creature that was under the mask which he wore, he would have been imprisoned, at the very least. Because he heeded his base passions instead of controlling them, he had become a beast, allowed to perpetrate against his wife, her daughter and her granddaughter. Because his wife would rather save face than confront him or live without him, she had become a slave to his wickedness and to her own vanity.

While Rosie's grandparents masqueraded themselves as worthy under the masks of their unchecked passions, she spoke against the abuse and the molestation and the deceit. Her grandmother threatened and blamed her. Her grandfather laughed at her. Rosie's parents may well have protected her from the abuse, but Rosie did not tell them about it until years later.

When she finally did learn of the abuse, her mother

confronted Bigdaddy. She spoke to him once on the phone and thereafter, she held her peace. When Rosie's father learned about the abuse, he stood idly by, nose stuck up in the air, doing nor saying anything of significance.

Rosie's mother had been molested by Bigdaddy, too, but she denied it for many years. Maybe she would have carried the secret of her molestation to the grave had it not been for Rosie, who when her grandfather offered her 20 dollars to have sex with him, told on him. She was 18 years old at the time. He told Rosie he could not stand to see her in misery and that he could "help her out." He said he had had sex with her mother before to "help her out." Rosie said she would not have sex with him, and she told her mother about his proposition.

She also asked her mother if it were true that he had asked her for sex or had had sex with her. Her mother hung her head down and said, "No," and that is all she said about it for years. Rosie asked her mother the same question again, after her divorce from an abusive man, after the birth of her children and after traveling to the "land of insanity" and back, "did he molest you?" This time her mother admitted that he had. The admission came too late to save

Rosie from some of the pits she had fallen into. It came in time to save her from some others.

When Bigmama heard about the 20-dollar sex proposition made by her husband to her granddaughter, she wept and wailed; she whooped and hollered. She cried, "Lawd Jesus." She carried on like she was the victim and as though Rosie had conspired with Bigdaddy to make her life more miserable than it already was.

She asked Rosie what she had done to provoke the proposition and what she felt her part was in that incident. Rosie reasoned that she had done nothing to provoke the proposition and that even if she had, Bigdaddy was the grandfather and he should have known better than to ask her for sex. Rosie told her grandmother that Bigdaddy had begun molesting her when she was in elementary school. Bigmama's final words on the matter were,

"Don't mention those things in my house again." Rosie never mentioned the molestation and proposition made by her grandfather again to her grandmother.

Sometimes on the nightly news, the anchors reported allegations of molestation made by children against their parents or other adults whom they knew. Bigdaddy would listen to the report, and after it was completed he would say,

"Those kids just lying. Nobody did nothin' to them."

Bigmama made no comment.

Rosie kept loving her grandparents, and she prayed for them and respected them until they died. But she did not spend much time with them. Being in their house was as an unspoken duty which she felt had to be performed. When she was discharged from her duty by their deaths, all was well with Rosie's soul. She was determined not to live the way they had taught her to live.

Rosie bundled up her bag of broken dreams, bound up her bleeding wounds and left home for a place unknown. With tears in her eyes, she began to chart new territory and forge new paths for new generations to follow.

Three

THE HOUSE BUILT ON
SINKING SAND

Rosie, now a young woman in her early 20's, rolled over in a bed that was not her own. The sun shone through a window attached to an apartment she had no financial responsibility for. Drug abuse, premarital sex and abortion had become part of her woeful lot. But in it all she reached for freedom. There was an uneasiness in the pit of her stomach, a dark foreboding of the judgment that would come crashing down upon her eventually if she did not change her life.

Kato came barreling into the room, skillfully singing

along with the reggae music that played in the background, "... Babylon system is the vampire, sucking the blood of the sufferers ...," sung Bob Marley in stereo. His voice hypnotized her with strange fear and magnetism.

"Are you still here," exclaimed Kato with a smile on his face. His words cut like a knife. Rosie knew she told him that she would be gone by 7:00 a.m. and it was now 8:17 a.m. Nevertheless, she felt rejection in his statement. She knew she did not belong "here." Yet every time she tried to break off this ungodly relationship, Kato countered with many reasons why they should remain as they were, non-committal, just sexual partners and friends. Because of her weakness of flesh, she relented. Each time Rosie left Kato's apartment, she left a piece of herself there. Now, there was not much of herself left.

He said he would marry her. He said he loved her and that she was a star. He said so many things, but the truth was that he meant her no good at all. He prostituted himself and she prostituted herself, and they were partners in the crime of their folly. They were as rudderless ships destined to crash on the rocks that lie surely ahead on their path of self-destruction. They were as two novices caught up in a whirlwind of passion, trying to love, yet having no true meaning of what love is.

As Rosie buried her head in the pillow to hide the tears that were on the verge of pouring out, Kato inched his way out of the bedroom, saying, "Peace and love to you." Then he walked out the front door. Rosie felt like an abandoned child, and she was.

The divorce of her parents, her mother's drinking habits, her father's elitist attitude and ambition, to name a few, were hindrances to her proper development. There was a breach in Rosie's foundation of security. Her estimate of self was diseased.

In a perfect world, we would have perfect parents raising perfect children. But we do not live in a perfect world. The degree of a woman's estimation of herself varies from, at best, one who acknowledges that she is growing in grace to, at worst, one who sells her soul for nothing. Rosie had grown into a woman who was dying spiritually, mentally and physically because of her sense of self-worthlessness.

She had learned to accept the fact that her parents could not offer her much solace in the area of her nagging pain. She did not like herself. She did not want to hear the bad thoughts that her mind spoke. She desperately needed someone to hold her, the one who understood the pain. But in her desire to be fulfilled, she continued to lose control of herself in destructive relationships. Rosie wanted to meet God face to face and complain directly to Him about her problems. Her foreparents had failed her, giving her only a legacy of pain and rejection. Their lives bore the false testimony that hope is futile. But Rosie had faith in salvation, a certain miraculous act that redeems people from the effects of past mistakes.

She wanted to know the one who had control over everything, and she wanted Him to fix her life. She was entangled in a myriad of sins, and she could not get loose. The evil gnawed at her flesh and burned her heart within. She desired freedom from the sin of fornication and low self-esteem and the nasty memories of molestation that pressed her down, but she could not let them go.

Rosie had a deep yearning in her heart that she believed was the call of God, beckoning her to Himself. No matter how she tried to evade the fundamentals of Christianity that somehow were imparted upon her by her family, even through their infidelity, her conscious was pricked, even in her own infidelity, that she owed a debt of faithfulness to her Creator.

She tried to loosen the shackles that held her bound, but it was of no use. She was stuck, just as stuck as a bear in a trap, stuck like a fly in a spider web. Because she was enslaved in the flesh, she went on a search for freedom in the spirit.

Four

NANA'S ALTAR

Rosie never saw anyone pray as much as she saw Nana pray. Nana, Rosie's paternal grandmother, had an altar in her bedroom with a statue on it. The statue stood about two and a half feet high. It was about one and a half feet wide and about eight inches in depth. It was a statue of Mary, the mother of Jesus, holding the heavy, lifeless body of her son, apparently after the crucifixion. The statue was bone white.

There were other items on the altar. There was a picture of one of the Catholic saints. He had a halo around his head and held three fingers up in what appeared to be a specific fashion. His eyes stared out from the picture as though meant to compel all onlookers to duty.

There was holy water in a container on the altar. Nana taught Rosie and her other grandchildren to dip the middle finger of the right hand in the holy water and make the sign of the cross by touching the forehead first, between the two breasts second, across the chest to the left shoulder area third and back across the chest to the right shoulder area fourth.

There were rosary beads on Nana's altar. She taught Rosie that as she held a bead of the rosary between her right index finger and thumb that she should say,

"Hail Mary, full of grace, the Lord is with thee. Blessed art thou among women, and blessed is the fruit of thy womb, Jesus." (Rosie was taught to bow her head when she said the name of Jesus.) "Holy Mary, mother of God, pray for our sins now and at the hour of our death."

The Rosary consisted of several beads and was separated by the chain which held the beads together in groups of beads. One was to say the above words to Mary from one bead to the next and from that bead to the next one until all the beads had been touched and spoken over.

Rosie's Nana was small in stature and very reserved. She often spent time with her grandchildren on Sundays.

Sometimes she would buy her granddaughters, Rosie and her cousin Winnie, matching outfits. The grandchildren always liked when their visits ended with a sundae or banana split from the local ice cream parlor.

Sometimes when Nana would drop Rosie and Winnie off at Winnie's home, Rosie would watch Nana walk away. She seemed so sad; she seemed so lonely.

There was contention between Rosie's father and his mother, Nana. There was a spirit of anger that most often attended their contact. Usually, Rosie's father aggressively opposed his mother while Nana responded with the question, "Why are you treating me this way?"

Nana was about 80 years old when she was "forced into retirement," as she put it. She did not want to stop working; she did not know what else she would do. At a retirement luncheon that was held in Nana's honor, Rosie learned many interesting things about her grandmother. She learned that her grandmother received a Master's degree in nursing. She learned that the cafeteria at Los Angeles General Hospital Nursing School was first integrated (allowing black people to eat therein) when her grandmother began her training.

Rosie was fascinated with the family history told to her by Nana. She wanted to know more. So she started talking to her grandmother about her life.

Nana had been a public health nurse. At some time in her career, she had been responsible for preparing young women in the clinic for abortions on the day the procedure would take place. Nana did not believe in abortion, so she would pray that the young women would change their minds and not go through with the procedure. As she prayed, she would sprinkle holy water in the corners of the abortion room before the clients were scheduled to come.

Nana was the first of two children born to her mother. She was raised in a Northern California community. Her mother was discriminated against because of her race and disallowed to get an adequate education. For survival's sake, she married Nana's father. The marriage did not last, "because," Nana said, "he was a mean man."

Nana's maternal grandmother was the daughter of a German immigrant father and a Cherokee Native mother. According to Nana, her grandmother favored her brother above her because Nana's complexion was less fair, and her hair was more kinky. Nana's maternal great grandfather, the

German, died at sea with his 12 sons on a fishing expedition. Nana's maternal grandfather, the man she described as the black man from "somewhere in Africa," was killed by a thief in the barber shop that he owned.

While Nana was attending Los Angeles City General Hospital Nursing School, she met a man. She was introduced to him by a friend. She thought he was really handsome and she said that is why she liked him and wanted to marry him. He did not feel the same way about her.

She said she begged and cried for him to marry her. Eventually, he consented. Nana's husband was a musician, and he also delivered the mail. Rosie never met him because he died before she was born. Her grandmother and father relayed painful memories to Rosie of her grandfather. She saw many photographs of her grandfather, and there was a painting of her grandparents on the wall in her grandmother's livingroom. One of her favorites stories, told to her by her father and his siblings, was about her grandfather once playing his saxophone in a band with Louis Armstrong.

The marriage between Nana and her husband was

rocky and abusive. Their many fights and separations sent the family up and down the highway between Oakland and Los Angeles.

Nana would run home with her children to her mother when the abuse was too much for her to handle, and she would go back to Los Angeles to her husband and near his family at other times. Sometimes the whole family, including Nana's husband lived in Oakland, and sometimes they all lived in Los Angeles.

Nana told Rosie that one late night, while she and her husband were lying in bed, her husband woke up and said to her, "I think I'll kill you tonight."

A struggle ensued. Nana got away and went to a neighbor's house. Her husband sent their eldest son, Rosie's father, to the neighbor to tell Nana if she did not come home he would kill all of the children.

Nana said she knew he would not kill the children, so she stayed at the neighbor's house and called the police. When the police came, she said, they took her husband and put him on a bus headed to Los Angeles.

While back in Los Angeles, recounted Nana, he suffered from diabetes-related complications and was hospitalized. Nana went to him at the hospital with their children. There they saw their father for the last time. Nana's husband asked her to go buy something for him from the store that day. When she came back to his room, he was deceased.

There was a major disagreement between Nana and Rosie's father about the way her grandfather had died. Nana contended he died in the hospital from diabetes-related complications. Her son contended that he was beaten by the police and suffered from injuries that took his life.

Shortly after the death of Nana's husband, she sent her 15-year-old son, Rosie's father, to the seminary. She said she and her husband had agreed that he should become a priest. Upon further reflection, she admitted that it was more her idea than her husband's. He had merely consented.

Nana said the administrators of the seminary would not allow her inside. She could only go as far as the outside lawn where they often had family visits while eating lunch.

Rosie's father never said much about his life in the seminary, only that while he was housed therein he developed a condition known as cluster headaches. On one of his visits home, Rosie's father told his mother that he was not going back to the seminary and he never did.

Nana had several statues and church symbols around her house and in her vehicle. She attended church on a daily basis. She said after the death of her husband she never wanted to marry another man, and she did not. But she was married to the church, in a sense. She even offered the church her eldest child, perhaps as a sacrifice for the redemption of her family. She was a faithful and loyal servant. Whether her church was as loyal to her still remains to be seen.

Five

THE WANDERING MIND

Rosie's father was an anti-Christian type of man. He once saw a bumper sticker on someone's car that read "Let Jesus Save You." He read it aloud so that Rosie could hear, and then he retorted, "Jesus couldn't save Himself." How's He going to save me?" Rosie's father believed that Christianity was the white man's way of controlling and enslaving black people.

He was not alone in his assessment. In fact, the dehumanization of black people through the institution of slavery and its Jim Crow successor made it hard for conscious people of African descent to accept Christianity as it was popularly preached. After all, America was a

"Christian" nation. Slave masters even quoted scriptures to their slaves. They said things like, "Servants, be subject to your masters with all fear; not only to the good and gentle, but also to the froward." (I Peter 2:18) Many of those "Christian" masters subjected their slaves to murder, rape, maiming, lynching, barter, and otherwise destroyed African American families and their chances for economic stability.

In order for the gospel to take root in their hearts, there was a question that first needed to be answered by truth-seeking, Bible-believing people of African American descent. The question is, how do we tap into the source of liberation promised by the gospel of Christ while conforming to the dictates of the so-called Christianity which appears to keep us enslaved?

In the wake of her own black consciousness, Rosie began to seriously doubt the power of Christ to save. Such doubt was erased only after she answered the question for herself. She found many answers in God's word. One of them is,

"Not every one that saith unto me, Lord, Lord, shall enter into the kingdom of heaven; but he that doeth the will of my Father which is in heaven. Many will say to me in that day, Lord, Lord, have we not prophesied in thy name? and in thy name done many wonderful works? And then will I profess unto them, I never knew you: depart from me, ye that work iniquity." (Matthew 7:21-23)

There are many beautiful cathedrals and storefront churches and preachers and priests and congregations of people who speak in the name of Christ but do not belong to Him. They are imposters. Their churches are dwelling places for foul spirits. They send forth doctrines as nets designed to enslave souls and destroy God's people.

One weekend when Rosie was visiting her father's house, she accidently saw him praying. She opened the bedroom door, and he was there, before the window on his knees. He was a bit perturbed that Rosie interrupted his prayer. Before that incident, Rosie did not even know her father prayed at all. She was glad to see him praying, but she wondered to whom he was praying.

Rosie's father told her that life is a continuous cycle yielding death powerless. He said that death was not to be feared. Rosie found courage against death in her father's statement, which, in effect sparked her belief in reincarnation. She was so courageous that she allowed herself to believe in things that to her "right-thinking" mind seemed impossible.

It was not as though her father formally guided her into mysticism, but he invited her away from Christianity and into a belief that, through some unexplained means, the power inherent in her "being" yielded death powerless. It resembled mysticism. She felt as though she had the gift of invincibility. But Rosie's father gave her no guidelines or instructions as to how she should use this "gift" he had revealed to her. Some say a little bit of knowledge is dangerous in the mind of a fool. Rosie found that the scanty information her dad had given her placed her as a wanderer on a stormy and ungodly spiritual path.

With the aid of the marijuana she smoked, Rosie became inordinately engrossed with spirituality outside of Christianity. She read about the Egyptian practice of worshiping the sun, and she tried it. Some Egyptians believed that the sun was the face of god, and she wanted to see it. One time she even tried to stare directly at the sun. When she squinted her eyes, she saw light emanating in four directions and forming a cross. When she opened her eyes wide, she saw two small, white disks over the pupils of her eyes. It was not until some time after the incident that she learned staring at the sun can surely cause blindness.

Ironically, years later, her father told her that if she wanted to give praise, that she should praise the sun which gives life and light and makes things grow. It was only then that Rosie believed that her father had been trying to guide her into worship of the sun from her early childhood.

In response to her sincere supplications, Rosie heard silence from the sun god. But she persisted in seeking its reply. She also became fascinated with other luminary bodies, the moon and the stars. She even saw lights flash before her eyes. Sometimes they hesitated as though they were trying to communicate with her. Sometimes they darted in and out of her vision. Their colors were red, white, blue, green and black.

On one occasion while she was in a state of meditation, she saw a white disk with hyphen-like line segments dissecting it on its border. She asked God that the disk would not move until she could count the dissecting line segments, and she counted them, and they were ten. On another occasion, while in conversation with her auntie, she saw a golf-ball-size, blue, luminous sphere levitating in the vicinity of where her auntie was sitting at the time.

Rosie's search into the spirit world intensified, and she became more distanced from her community and the society at large. It was as though she were caught between two worlds, and she had no desire to go back to reality as she had known it from childhood. While in this aimless utopian state, she was introduced to Siddha Meditation, a discipline born in the Eastern philosophy of India and governed by a guru.

The guru's name was Swami Muktananda, and she saw his picture on the cover of a book in the library. As she looked at the book, the eyes of the picture of the guru seemed to come to life and hypnotize Rosie. Her face literally began to assume a circular motion as though it were spinning around the axis of her nose. She looked intently at the guru's eyes. Then she opened the book and read it and believed everything it said.

Rosie found the Siddha Foundation in her city and she visited it. It was called an Ashram. People sat in the atmosphere of a blue, candle-lit room chanting Indian words and smelling the Nag Champa incense that burned. They called it Blue Pearl incense. The "blue pearl" was the object of meditation, whatever it was. It looked like the blue light she saw while in conversation with her auntie.

One day Rosie entered the Ashram and followed a silent beckoning to a small room. The room was lit with a blue glow created by the blue candles that burned therein. There were also pillows, burning incense, a small digital clock and a huge picture of Swami Muktananda hanging from the wall in this room. Rosie did not quite know what she was doing or who she was worshiping, but she sat down on the pillows as she sought to be engulfed in the flame of at-one-ment with God.

As she sat, drifting on the vibrations created by the aimless state of her senses, a man entered the small room. He bowed down to the huge picture of Swami Muktananda. Rosie, believing he knew what he was doing, followed in kind and bowed down to the picture of Swami Muktananda, also. It was upon her rising from bowing down to a picture of a man that could not move that she was awakened out of her stupor.

"Where am I," she thought. Although she had been wandering in her mind, something from the depths of her being reminded her that the huge picture of the Indian man she was now bowing herself down to was not God. She thought,

. "That man must have been some kind of a fool, bowing down to a picture of a man." Then she said to herself out loud,

"And I must be a fool, too."

Rosie walked out of the darkness of the Ashram. As she looked across the street where there stood two edifices, Star Bethel Baptist Church and Your Black Moslem Bakery, Rosie said to herself,

"What is the truth, and where can I find God"?

Rosie suffered numerous encounters with false spiritual teachers. Each one feasted upon her soul, and her spirit was badly mutilated. She had almost forgotten who she was. Many of her family members thought she was crazy. She had come to a point where she could muster up a semblance of strength, and with it she went to see her dad. She believed he could help bring her out of the confused state in which she found herself. Rosie's father invited her into his home, he and his brand new wife.

In the best way she could, Rosie attempted to show him how broken she was. She explained about the molestation that took place when she was in the care of her mother after the divorce. She tried to talk to him about her spirituality, but she felt like such a bumbling idiot in the presence of his high authority and insight. After all, he had a PhD in Political Science.

He acted like he knew everything, and she, being his daughter, believed he did. She tried to talk to him and glean from him how she should regain her sanity. He would be her last hope, she thought. He was her daddy.

She held, as it were, her trembling hand out to him. It was as though she were dangling on a tight rope above a black hole and he was standing on solid ground. He did not take her hand, he nor his new wife. Rosie was devastated, and she fell into the black hole of temporary insanity.

S ix

REACHING FOR THE LIGHT

Rosie was admitted into a mental hospital where through group therapy, one-on-one psychotherapy and other techniques, she learned how to cope with her life as it was. She learned how to play the hand of cards she had been dealt. When she got out of the hospital, Rosie was not totally healed, but she was well enough to function with certain restrictions.

As Rosie continued to wander and search, she heard a sound. It was a dreadful, hypnotizing sound coming from the air waves over the radio. A recording artist named Gil Scott Heron described it as "storm music." It was music that spoke of the evils against the oppressed of the world and the love of God for His people. Rosie had been oppressed since she could remember, so she truly believed that the musicians were singing directly to her. Since her search was for God, she listened to the music intently to see if He had sent a word for her, in full anticipation that He would encapsulate a personal message for her in these very songs.

They called it Reggae music. The message was potent enough to keep Rosie's mind pondering for years. But the message inside the music was even more powerful.

Bob Marley was a popular Reggae musician, and there were others, too, like Peter Tosh, Bunny Wailer, Hugh Mundell and Steel Pulse, to name a few. When they sang and played their music, it was as if Rosie's character was being vindicated. They promised that the wicked would be eradicated from the face of the earth, and in their place would stand the righteous.

The message was solid. Many of the lyrics came directly from the Bible. It was from listening to the Reggae music, that scales of blindness began to fall from Rosie's eyes. Some of the vocalists sang about Babylon as a system that seeks to destroy God's people. They were mostly talking about the tribes of black people scattered throughout the earth, but the music had world-wide appeal. It was as if pieces of an unsolved puzzle which was Rosie's life were coming together. She began to know that she was a child of God and that He knew her and cared for her personally.

The words of the pure message of Reggae music, those words that came from the Bible and those words which spoke of the righteous overcoming the wicked were as meat to Rosie, and she was well-fed. However, the people whom she met who made and professed the music she loved so dearly, for the most part, did not live according to the purity of the message.

Rosie's boyfriend, Kato, was a Reggae recording artist, but he was no model for a child of God. He sang about the love of Jah, but he fornicated. He smoked and sold ganja (marijuana), and he had multiple relationships and too many children, all of which he was ill-prepared to care for. He did not even try to care for them. Kato's fellowship of friends were just like him.

Rosie thought she might have done just as well to have kept bowing to the picture of Swami Muktando as believing in the messages in the Reggae music she loved so dearly. She felt she had come no closer to God than when she had begun to ally herself with Him.

"The only way out of this," she thought to herself, "is death, the death of who I am."

"I got it," she continued, "I'll separate what is good in me from what is bad."

But she could not tell what was good and what was bad. It was all mixed up. She feared if she cut away what she thought was the wrong thing, she might rid herself of the right thing. She was confused.

Her struggle with the unseen forces that held her bound was maddening. She would not be able to hold out much longer. Something would have to give. The knowledge of sin and her being stuck therein was eating her alive.

She wanted to let go of sin, but she could not. Sin lived inside of her and took good care of itself. Rosie was trapped, and it was as though hellfire was in the pit of her stomach. Yet from the depths of her groaning and reasoning she heard the voice of the Beloved. It was a calm voice, small and still. He said,

"Freedom from sin requires a sacrifice. Lay yourself

down on the altar and become dead if you want to know. Gaze at your fruitless actions through the eyes of the Spirit which compels you, beckoning you to live above what you now know."

S even
===

DELIVERANCE

Then she met the man that would have destroyed her if it had not been for the mercy of God. He had many names. Some people on the streets called him Cookie. He called himself Master. He allowed Rosie to call him Exalted. He told Rosie that he had only a short time to live, and he asked her if she would marry him to help make his remaining days on earth pleasant. Rosie married him. It was a trap.

At the outset of their relationship, Cookie told Rosie that there were no grounds for divorce. Then he proceeded to beat her. He accused her of having affairs with other men or lusting after them, and he terrorized, raped and beat her. When he was feeling especially exalted he would tell her she was a liability not an asset. Sometimes he would ask her,

"Why don't you just leave."

But if she tried to leave him, he would compel her to stay. He would beat her emotionally, physically and psychologically. He tried to bind her spiritually as he sought to enjoin Islam upon her, asserting that it was the only righteous religion, especially for black people.

Cookie was not rotten-to-the-core bad. He had some good qualities. He would sing and write music. He also wrote essays and poetry. He could make people laugh, and he had redemptive and lofty ideas about freedom for the human race, especially for black people. Maybe his positive ideas would have influenced him to act right had he not been trapped and overcome in a cycle of abuse and doing a dance that his genetic make-up, his upbringing and his free choice commanded that he do.

He was self-centered and self-destructive. If he could not break the cycle of abuse for himself, there would be no hope for Rosie's redemption in his heart. The image that he held of women, specifically, the wife, had somehow become corrupted in his mind. He wanted love and security and understanding, inordinately so.

As it is with most men, Cookie had a "manly" need that only a woman could fill. Yet because he chose unhealthy relationships, he often found himself seeking another woman to replace the one that had just gotten away. He preferred that his "significant other" care for him, somewhat as a mother cares for her child. Yet he was an unruly and disrespectful child, flying into a rage at his would-be mother whenever she did not obey his often unreasonable commands.

Besides the fact that a wife was never meant to be her husband's mother, Rosie did not have the tools to even pretend she could ever serve in that capacity. She was in such desperate need herself. In fact, she was looking for her husband to father her. Their marriage was destined for failure. Cookie was looking for Rosie to supply his needs, and Rosie was looking for Cookie to supply her needs, and both of them were as dry, empty deserts, devoid of the wherewithal to supply their own needs, singly.

At times, when Rosie could have easily walked away physically, from their marriage, she realized that she was chained by fear and remorse for her past sins. Furthermore, she and Cookie had two small children. In Rosie's mind, a family was supposed to stay together even if the mother was chosen as the dying sacrifice for the family's salvation.

The spirit within her, the joy she had in the knowledge that she would some day know God, was replaced with a spirit of heaviness and shame. Cookie was like a brick wall across her path to liberation. But she kept on praying. As she washed his shirts and pants by hand she prayed. As she hung them out to dry she prayed. As she cut, washed and prepared the chicken they ate together she prayed.

One early morning when she thought she was dreaming, Rosie saw a vision. From her bed, there was a window to her left and a window behind her. In her state of semi-consciousness, she saw what appeared to be a wooly, white lamb or llama peering at her from behind the bars that were over the windows. The lamb startled her as one of his eyes stared at her intently. Frightened, she turned away from the lamb's gaze. Then the lamb peered at her through the bars of the windows behind her.

Just then, she had a vision of her husband standing in the bathroom with one foot on the lidded toilet stool and one foot on the floor. He had no shirt on and a pair of shorts or pants on the bottom. He was brushing his teeth while looking in the mirror of the medicine cabinet.

When Rosie awoke to full consciousness, her husband was not in bed. She went to the bathroom, and there he was in the exact position he had been in the vision. He was dressed the same way and doing exactly the same thing, the lighting in the bathroom showing forth the same scene Rosie had witnessed with her eyes closed, and she rejoiced. She knew a messenger had come to her in the form of the lamb to proclaim her liberation from this very abusive man.

Rosie was so happy that she insisted that Cookie and she pray. He marveled at her joy. He smiled and complied. They prayed in the Moslem tradition, on prayer rugs, he on his red one and she on her green one. They assumed the prayer positions taught in Islam to be used when doing obeisance to God. Rosie was so excited that she continued on in prayer, using prayer positions more than the prescribed repetitions for that particular prayer time (Prayer is prescribed five times a day in Islam).

Cookie brought to her attention that they had

fulfilled the requirement, so they stopped doing Islamic obeisance, but she continued to praise God. Had Cookie only known what was in her mind, maybe he would have beaten her half to death right then, or maybe he would have brought her some flowers and begged her to stay. God only knows. Rosie knew that she was free, and she waited patiently for God to perform His great act that would allow everybody else to see that she was free.

Months before Rosie's vision, Cookie had been arrested. The arrest took place on the night of his birthday. For some reason, Cookie believed it was his appointed duty every year to congratulate himself or mourn over his life (only he knew which) on his birthday. He got pissy drunk on his each and every birthday. In an effort to keep Cookie from getting drunk on this particular birthday, Rosie decided to give him a party, cook food and invite his family home for dinner.

Cookie consented to accompany Rosie and their children to the grocery store so they could shop for the party. While Rosie shopped alone with her children, Cookie was somewhere else. She later found out that he was in the bar celebrating his birthday. After a day not so happily spent, Rosie trying to prepare a party for her husband by herself while he slowed her down with his slurred speech, dizziness and self-aggrandizement, she fell from exhaustion onto a big pillow on the livingroom floor. Cookie was swaggering drunk then. The pissy part was soon to follow.

He grabbed his big wooden walking stick from the corner and said he was going out for a while. Rosie tried to warn him that in his state of inebriation, maybe it would have been better had he stayed home. In a form that was true to his folly, he declined her offer and he went out that evening, the sun soon to set. Rosie believed before he left that evening he would end up in trouble. After all, he could hardly see.

Cookie did get in trouble. He broke a man's jaw that night and landed in jail. If he had stayed home, maybe it would have been Rosie's jaw. Praise God for his salvation and for miracles. Cookie claimed he did not break the man's jaw. A jury of his peers found him guilty.

When it came time for Cookie to pay the penalty for his crime of assault and battery, he was given the opportunity to serve in Work Release.

When the time drew near for Cookie to be remanded

to the sheriff, he terrorized Rosie. He hated the fact that he was going into custody and she would remain free. He threatened to kill her. He raped her. He tortured her mentally. He purchased and smoked crack cocaine in lieu of buying food and soap and the like.

Then one day he was gone. Her redemption was very near. Rosie could breathe a breath of fresh air now. She had space to be. She was not being beaten down with every step she took.

But though Cookie was housed in the Work Release facility, he violated its rules by making visits home to bother Rosie many mornings. He wanted to check on her and to keep her in check. She did not know what she would do. Would she leave him? Where would she go? Was it right for a woman to divorce a man even though she is the mother of his two children?

Rosie was invited to a birthday party at a family restaurant which was right across the street from the Work Release facility in which Cookie was housed every night. Cookie asked his mother where Rosie and the children were that day, and his mother told him, not intending to facilitate the asinine actions that followed. When Cookie showed up at the restaurant, fire was in his eyes. He accused Rosie of having some type of sexual dealings with a man which stood near her. The man was her cousin. Actually, the man was more like her uncle since he was her mother's cousin, nearly the same age as her mother.

Cookie invited Rosie outside and proceeded to hit and knock her down to the ground. She knew her mother and cousin and others were right in the restaurant. They were sitting right by the window when she left, but not one of them helped her. She battled that demon with the help of God alone and she felt all alone.

Cookie told Rosie to give him his kids and the keys to his car and apartment. He proposed that Rosie just disappear into the sunset and start a new life or something. Who knows what his wandering mind was thinking. He snatched up their children, packed them in the family car and drove around with them for a while. When Cookie's foolishness finally gave way to reason, he realized he had to check into the Work Release facility at a time certain. He returned the car with the children in it to Rosie, but he retained its keys and the key to the apartment. Rosie walked with her small children to the Work Release facility, demanded her keys, drove to the apartment, packed her bags and left, leaving the keys to the apartment inside. She would return the next day to leave the car and its keys.

Rosie called the Work Release authorities and told them what Cookie had done, how he knocked her down and hit her while he was a Work Release participant. After having assured Rosie that they would "put the fear of God" into Cookie, the authorities put him in jail. Rosie heard that when Cookie got out of custody he broke all the windows out of the apartment they lived in together. Cookie was still a tortured soul, and Rosie had become free.

Sometimes Rosie would see Cookie in different places, at home when he would come to get the children for a visit or, rarely, in passing. She spent a day with him one time after their divorce, on a family outing. She thought it would be good for the children. He tried to manipulate and control and constrain her like she was his very own mule. She never got too close to him again.

But Rosie sent a prayer out for him. She prayed that God would reach beyond the layers of rubble that had enclosed him and birth the soul inside longing so desperately to be free.

E ight

GOD SENT AN ANGEL

Rosie had been rudely interrupted by a bad marriage to a rude man, but she refused to give up her life's goal, to really know God. Rosie arose at 4:00 a.m. many mornings, sometimes at 3:00 a.m., to pray and meditate and read.

Rosie tried to know God. She reached with all of her might to touch Him. The power of sin might well have lost its grip, but the guilt of sin tricked her. It told her she could be perfect if she tried hard enough. As she reached for perfection, she saw how imperfect she was. She wanted to please God with her being. She wanted to sacrifice her life for Him. But she felt unworthy. Daily she rehearsed to herself that she was not good enough for God. She was dulling her ear to His forgiveness and killing her hopes to trust Him until God sent an angel to Rosie. He pointed her to the Savior.

The angel did not look like an angel at all. He looked like a man. But he was a special man. His name was Timothy. Some called him Tim. Timothy never claimed to be an angel, but he did bear a special message from God. Tim was at peace, and it seemed as though he genuinely cared for Rosie. Rosie became reacquainted with Tim when he knocked on the front door of her apartment on a day which had, up to that point, been quite uneventful. His visit was a surprise. Rosie and Tim had actually been friends when they were teenagers, but now they were grown-up, and there were many new things to tell one another.

Timothy and Rosie began their visit in the middle of the afternoon, and it was not complete until very late that night. They talked and they ate dinner together. The meal was good, but the conversation was even better. Tim had something important to tell Rosie. He had come to tell her about God's intentions for her. He had come as a messenger in answer to her prayer. He showed her passages of scripture in her own Bible, and he said something to her that was most profound. He said, "Jesus is coming again, soon."

Rosie did not know if she had heard that before, though it sounded familiar to her. It seemed as though she had heard somewhere that Jesus was coming to the earth a second time. When she heard this news she believed that Jesus' emergence from the heavens was of the utmost importance. The words which Tim spoke had merit. And what if Jesus did come again? What would that mean to her?

When Timothy left very late that night he left Rosie with the assurance of comfort and peace. He did not leave her empty like others had done in the past. He filled her with the promise that God loves her. He assured her of the limitless care of Jesus the Savior. He offered her a vision for guidance. Timothy loved her with a tender and healing love, God's love. He pointed her in the direction of the Messiah, and then he departed.

Rosie considered the Messiah, and she read the Bible. After a period of prayer and study, Rosie began to know Jesus. She no longer saw Him as the white man in a picture, but she knew Him as an ever-present friend. The words that Timothy spoke about Jesus and pointed out in the Bible about Him were sustained, not as a sound that reverberates in the inner ear and is trapped in the mind as a memory, but as an impulse which is continually refreshed from its source. Rosie had come to accept that Jesus lives. She could not help but love Him.

Timothy spoke straight and answered questions she did not even verbally ask. It was as though a line of communication had been opened between the Most High God and her, and the name of Jesus was familiar to her, just as familiar as it had been in her youth. Rosie's faithfulness was rewarded by the Spirit of God. She had been given the ability to see herself in a different way. She no longer defined herself as an abused ex-wife, disrespected ex-girlfriend, molested child and otherwise confused and guilty human being. She was now a person whom God loves.

N ine

THE ENCOUNTER

After having secured her children in the care of a friend, Rosie was on her way to a party one evening. At about 10:00 o'clock p.m., she heard a knock on the door.

"Who's that," she thought, a bit startled by the unexpected intrusion. When she opened the door, Tim was standing on her front porch.

Several weeks had gone by since Rosie's long meeting with Tim. She thought about him often. She did not know his phone number, and she wanted to contact him. Now, he was at her door. He told her that he was in the neighborhood and had decided to visit her.

Rosie was very glad to see Tim. She welcomed him into her home and turned on some of the lights.

"Man," she thought in a downcast inner voice, "I can't tell him where I'm going. I know he cannot approve of it."

Tim's approval was important to Rosie. She decided not to tell him that she was going anywhere. She was convicted by her knowledge that going to the party was not good for her and arrested by Tim's presence. She knew that she could save face if she sat down, got comfortable and denied herself leave to go to the party. Maybe God had come to her spiritual rescue by sending Tim. Now she would not waste her time at a party looking for love in a lusty environment. God had sent her a friend to love right to her doorstep, and that's all; they were only friends.

The focus of Tim's coming to visit Rosie that night was to bring her an invitation to his church for a "Community Guest Day." Rosie accepted the invitation.

~

Rosie arrived at Timothy's church on time. The atmosphere was warm and energetic. There was the smell of food in the air. Music was playing, and the people were very happy. Rosie was greeted warmly and then directed to a seat by an usher. The speaker of the hour was a woman.

Her name was Letta Beacon.

The Minister wore her mostly grey hair trimmed into a neat afro. She wore small horn-rimmed glasses which had a chain attached, and she could look over the tops of her glasses. She was about 5' 5" and a little bit plump. The flowing dress that she wore was made of a floral print fabric. She spoke in a deep and powerful voice. She wore no make-up or jewelry to embellish herself, yet there was a glow of compelling beauty about her. As she stood up to speak, the choir began to sing "The Lord is in his Holy Temple," and she dropped to her knees and prayed aloud. She rose up to speak, and after a few preliminary comments and warm greetings to the congregation she preached a sermon.

~

"A woman met Jesus," began the minister. "She was frail and weak with desire. Yet she was strengthened by her appointment with Jesus one day at Jacob's well. Thirst drew her to the well. Yet she could not fully realize the significance of this encounter until He touched her.

"He said to the woman, 'Give me to drink.' John 4:7.

"He touched her. It was warm and deep. It was not

on the surface. It was not a physical touch. He peeled away the soiled garments one by one until she stood before Him, one discovered, as naked as in the day that He called her forth from the darkness of the womb. She was not physically naked, but her mind was laid totally bear. He had access to the inside."

Rosie perked up in her seat; her eyes were focused with great interest toward the minister.

"He wanted her, but not the flesh," continued the minister.

"He wanted to open her mind. Now He had her full attention. She was compelled and stayed, as one beholding her face in a mirror for the very first time.

"She, being a Samaritan and He being a Jew, she felt as rebuked in His eyes. Yet He said to her,

"'If thou knewest the gift of God, and who it is that saith to thee, Give me to drink; thou wouldest have asked of him and he would have given thee living water.' John 4 :10

"He said He would give her living water which would be a well-spring of life flowing inside of her, 'springing up into everlasting life.' John 4:14.

"She wanted the water, and she boldly asked Him for

it. But He did not give it to her just then. He wanted her to go tell someone. This would not be as bread eaten in secret. He wanted her to make known to the men this beneficent act. His gift would be given only after the woman told someone else about Him."

"Amen," shouted a lone voice from the congregation.

"'Jesus said to her, Go, call thy husband, and come hither. John 4:16,'" continued the minister.

"Relationships with others is key to our relationship with Christ. The query is set forth in the Bible, How can a person love God whom he has not seen and hate those which are with him on a daily basis? The living water and relationship Jesus offered this woman was somehow connected with the relationship that the woman had with her husband.

"Good parental relationships teach obedience, adherence to law and order and point to the direction of the soul's flight. When growing up in the household of our parents, we are inspired to aim for our life's goal, which promises the reward of love. The marriage relationship, on the other hand, is love in action. It is a relationship wherein two consenting adults agree to become as a house built for security."

Rosie sat in silence, her heartbeat quickening, as the minister seemed to be massaging her damaged emotions. The minister continued.

"The marriage relationship engenders trust, faith and creativity and sanctifies the soul's communion with the Creator much like a house protects from predators on the outside thereof so that those that dwell on the inside may perpetuate life therein. It is companionship which aids the sojourning soul in reaching with all of its might to the reward of eternal life. God said in the beginning, 'It is not good for man to be alone.' Read Genesis 2:18.

"Marriage is the dwelling wherein the human spirit is unwrapped of many trappings. Marriage admits the married into the inner recesses of the mind and body to soar to the heights, depths, breadths and lengths of the awesome power of God's love.

"Marriage is a special place in creation. It is a life-long agreement between a man and a woman. The marriage relationship is like the covenant between God and His people, or more importantly, God and the believing soul, personally.

"Amen" echoed through the sanctuary as a syncopated chorus. Interested congregants waved fans and clapped their hands. The minister continued.

"Jesus said to the woman, 'Go, call thy husband, and come hither.'

"Oftentimes young women and men reach the age of consent and instead of seeking the voice of God to guide them and point them in the direction of life, they seek the significant other in an attempt to fulfill their need for companionship and to fulfill the call of God. And when the young man and woman find one another, if not in Christ, they oftentimes destroy one another.

"Contrary to popular opinion, marriage is much more than a sexually fulfilling living arrangement between a man and woman that breeds security and creates a place in society for the two who are joined as one. It is actually a place established with authority, dominion and power over the earth. It is the place from whence two become one and work together to be fruitful, multiply, replenish and subdue the earth 'and have dominion over the fish of the sea, and over the fowl of the air, and over every living thing that moveth upon the earth. Genesis 1:28.'"

"All right, now," shouted Rosie, wiping a small tear drop from the corner of her eye. The minister continued.

"The authority God gave to the man and woman over the earth was given to them in and through the covenant relationship of marriage. Marriage is earth's first institution. It is the institution upon which all other institutions are based. And it is the institution which has been most rankled by attacks from the devil in an attempt to annihilate the human race. Having a correct view of the marriage relationship allows us to see the threat to the life of the human race as marriage suffers from the syndrome of its intended destruction, i.e., fornication, adultery, abortion, divorce, spousal abuse, child abuse and molestation, homosexuality, et cetera.

"The Hebrew word for marriage means to be fruitful, in thought, word and deed and to increase in the earth in all respects, to fulfill the plan of God, to excel, enlarge, grow up, to nourish, to gather together, fulfill, furnish, satisfy and have wholly, to tread down and subjugate and bring into bondage, or subdue the earth."

"Hallelujah," shouted a lone voice in the

congregation. The minister continued.

"Knowing the awesome task of husband and wife to fulfill the meaning of the word "marriage," is it little wonder that those who take the marriage covenant so lightly are those that often find themselves in a quagmire of sinfulness, spiraling downwards with nauseating speed?

"Jesus said to the woman, 'Go bring thy Husband.' She wanted the water of life, which satisfies. And Jesus said, 'Go bring thy Husband.'

"'And Adam said, This is now bone of my bones, and flesh of my flesh: she shall be called Woman, because she was taken out of Man. Therefore shall a man leave his father and his mother, and shall cleave unto his wife: and they shall be one flesh.' Genesis 2:23 and 24.

"What is this life in which a man would leave his father and mother and cleave to his wife, the parents having housed and fed and taught their child and pointed him in the right direction so that he may live and not die? Death is the cessation of life. But what is life? Is it the state in which we are perpetually guarding from its cessation, or is it the state of perpetual creativity and joy? Many of us realize little more of life than subsistence, fighting the hunger pangs, appeasing the bill collectors and keeping a stiff upper lip in the face of sorrow. But what is life? Is it constantly guarding the flame from the menacing storm, or is it warming oneself in its glow?"

Someone in the congregation said, "Hmm," loudly, as if to underscore the minister's question.

"The woman who met Jesus at the well wanted the joy of life," continued the minister.

"In obedience to the cultural dictates of the circumstances surrounding the encounter -- Jesus was a Jew; she was a Samaritan, Jesus was a man; she was a woman -- she attempted to comply with the mores of her time and not engage in a conversation with a Jewish male at Jacob's well.

"But Jesus wanted to bless this woman; He wanted to give her life. He knocked at the door of her heart, and she let Him in and continued to engage in a discourse that was seemingly, because of their different genders and nationalities, inappropriate. She was willing to let down the guard that would separate her from Jesus because she truly wanted the living water that He offered. The woman at Jacob's well exhibited holy desire, which is the flame that we protect from the storms of life that threaten to quench it.

She was willing to shed the trappings of cultural law in order to be touched by the hand of the Master.

"Jesus said to the woman, 'Go, call thy husband, and come hither.'

"'Husband ... Husband ... Husband ... Husband ... Husband ... '

"The word reverberated through her mind five times. She remembered five husbands. Maybe he was able to quench her thirst for a time, but each in his turn was relieved of his service of being her husband. He could have been eaten up by his love for strong drink or beaten her to the point of causing her to run away. Maybe he was an adulterer and his lust for strange women drove her away."

Rosie's eyes were wide open. She clung to the minister's every word on the edge of her seat. "Is she talking to me?" thought Rosie.

"Maybe the woman, herself, was unstable. Possibly the husband did not please her and she left him for another and left the other for yet another and so on. There are a myriad of possibilities for her multiple divorces, but this one thing we know; Jesus knew her past, He knew her present, and He was beckoning her to her glorious future.

He would cause to flow this well-spring of water from within her only after she acknowledged to someone else, her husband, that He was the Christ, the one having power to make her whole."

"But I don't have a husband," cried out Rosie. Her cry was loud, but it banged like a ping-pong ball against the walls of her mind until it came to rest and she heard nothing but the minister's words." The minister continued.

"The heavenly Father espoused his daughter, the woman, to his son, the man, and they were made perfect. In fact, the act of giving the man and the woman to one another was their perfection. The prime root for the Hebrew word which means bride is a word which means, to complete or make perfect. As Jesus magnified the marital situation of the Samaritan woman at Jacob's well, He magnified the point that she had failed miserably in being made perfect in marriage or perfecting her husband(s) in marriage.

"The gift of life that Jesus offered to the woman at Jacob's well is the gift of life He offers to all. It is the fruit of salvation. It is the nectar of life, sweeter than the honey and the honey comb. (Psalms 19:10) It is the inside that we guard with marriage to protect from annihilation on the outside. Without the gift of the living water that Christ offered to the woman at Jacob's well, that He offers to all who will partake of it, all of our efforts in sanctifying the most intimate of our relationships are in vain.

"It appears as though Jesus may have been saying to this woman at Jacob's well that she was barred from receiving the water of life if she was unmarried or could not convince her husband to come to Jesus, because immediately upon her asking for the water of life for which He had suggested she ask, He said,

"'Go, call thy husband, and come hither.' John 4:16.

Some men in the congregation shouted out, "Amen." A round of giggles rippled through the sanctuary. The minister smiled and waited until the laughter subsided, and then she continued.

"Marriage between a man and a woman is meant to be a fulfilling and pleasurable relationship, and between the fiery darts of the devil's rage that the marriage institution suffers on a constant basis, it can be. It is a saving relationship. Faithfulness in marriage protects the body from the diseases that can be brought about through multiple sexual partners. Faithfulness in marriage helps to guard the soul from loneliness. Marriage is the foundation of the family and tribe and society, securing the soul attached therein in an earthly habitation and in emotional health. And, yes, the survival of the soul is dependent upon the marriage relationship. Does this mean, then, that unmarried people shall be lost and without hope if they never marry? No, absolutely not!

"Again, the marriage relationship between a man and a woman is a type of marriage relationship between Christ and his bride, the church. Jesus was not married into an earthly marriage, but He was a man. He was the best man that ever lived. Jesus was making known to this woman at Jacob's well the experience of a covenant relationship with Christ, the relationship on the inside of the heart, protected from her sinfulness and her instability.

"In repentance and acknowledgment of her failure or sin, she would be free to enter into the covenant relationship with Christ, and so would the five husbands. And the covenant relationship with Christ supersedes the marriage relationship. In this covenant, Christ is the husband and the church is His bride. Christ is the Lord, and the woman or man that enters into a covenant with Him is the beloved. The Lord says to the unmarried woman,

"'Sing, O barren, thou that didst not bear; break forth into singing, and cry aloud, thou that didst not travail with child: for more are the children of the desolate than the children of the married wife, saith the Lord . . . For thy Maker is thine husband; the LORD of hosts is his name; and thy Redeemer the Holy One of Israel; The God of the whole earth shall he be called.' Isaiah 54:1 and 5.

"And the Lord says to the unmarried man,

"'. . . neither let the eunuch say, Behold, I am a dry tree. For thus saith the LORD unto the eunuchs that keep my Sabbaths, and take hold of my covenant; Even unto them will I give in mine house and within my walls a place and a name better than of sons and of daughters: I will give them an everlasting name, that shall not be cut off.' Isaiah 56:3-5.

"When the woman knew this was the Christ with whom she spoke, she was touched, and she was changed. She left her water pot, the empty water pot, the water pot that had outlived its usefulness, the water pot that, though it had contained much water, could not satisfy her soul. Now, she would be filled by the well-spring of living water.

"'She went her way to the City and said to the men,

"'Come, see a man, which told me all things that ever I did: is not this the Christ?' John 4:29"

~

The minister took off her glasses and stretched her arms wide. With a big smile on her face she invited whosoever would to enter into a covenant with Jesus saying,

"Won't you come?"

To Rosie, it was as though Minister Beacon knew her life. She had answers to so many questions. Rosie was moved to the point of a passionate letting of tears. Her body shook uncontrollably as she placed her hands over her face and wept long and hard. It was but a short time before three or four ladies came as angels, wiping her tears with tissue and fanning her with paper fans and hugging her. She was as a traveler that had been on a long journey away from home, far away from God.

Rosie wanted to embrace the Divine. Her arms had been full of sinfulness but now they were open. This time, she would not settle for less than her portion, the portion that the Creator made available for all of His children, that which tends to life. She would not fold her arms about herself in self-pity and loneliness, but she would remain supple and await her appointment with the Father. He would show her the way. She felt the pain of anticipation and the pain of deceitful lusts warring against her flesh, parading themselves as the blessing of God. But through her faith in the word of God she waited for the true blessing.

Rosie had been as light as a feather, and she blew with the wind, wherever it would go. To Rosie, blowing in the wind or rolling like a stone, aimlessly, was freedom. She was learning, however, that freedom of this sort was leading her to certain destruction. She had no control of where the wind would take her as it whispered in her ear, "Let's play," and the wind made no promises for her future.

Rosie knew that she had a primary work to accomplish for her own healing. Yet because of her desire to have someone hold her and cradle her in his arms of security, she had cast her fate to chance, hoping that some man somewhere would feel it was his appointed duty to plant her in his garden and tend to her growth.

But rolling stones and blowing leaves do not collect in well-planned schemes. They end up in dead ends and garbage heaps. It would be up to Rosie to have a goal, aim for it and walk along the path of her aim to an expected end. Surely· being a wife was a laudable goal, and that was Rosie's foremost dream, but before her dream would be fully realized, Rosie had to know herself. She would have to reach beyond reacting to the negative actions perpetrated against her to acting on her own behalf, despite the opposition that she had experienced or ever would experience.

T^{en}

ONE DAY AT DAY CARE RAFIKI

It was a warm, Spring day. Rosie placed her key in the locked door of a white and yellow cottage. As she turned the door knob, she got a bit excited. She would embark upon another day's journey into the land of interaction with the little people. Rosie's own children and the children and staff at Day Care Rafiki were her closest family. Each weekday morning at 5:30 a.m. she would arrive from her one-bedroom apartment to a world of wonder in the day care. Here, she and the children and the other teachers would explore the nations, the beauty of nature and the joy of song. Here in the day care, she and the children and the other teachers would get their hands wet in paint and muddy in the garden and sticky with glue. Here they would experience comfort and tranquility as they unfolded their cots and slept for their afternoon naps.

From the day care they would travel to beaches where they would get their feet wet and sand between their toes. They would collect sea shells and take photographs. They would hike along the trails of the inland areas and inhale the pungent aromas of eucalyptus and pine. They would sit by the lakes and throw rocks and eat lunches and dream.

It was a short while after four or five of the early students had arrived that Savannah walked in the front door of the day care. She was dressed artistically, as usual, in her most unique style, but there was something very different about her face and her walk. It was as though she had been carrying a heavy load and had carried it as far as she could. Upon her entrance to the day care, she wept profusely and bitterly. Rosie met Savannah at the door and embraced her. The bodies of both of the women shook with Savannah's overwhelming grief. The children ran, calling,

"Sister Savannah, Sister Savannah," some of them with their arms around her legs, some touching on her thighs and belly.

Rosie, gently pulling the children away, said quietly, "Sister Savannah will be okay." She beckoned one of the older children to keep an eye on the younger ones at the free play area. Then Rosie escorted Savannah into the sitting room. Both of the women sat on the love seat. Savannah's heaving and outburst of tears rocked them back and forth.

After what seemed to have been a very long time but was actually about five minutes, Savannah spoke to Rosie.

"Did you read yesterday's newspaper," Savannah said, her voice quivering and weak.

"No, I did not," answered Rosie. "What happened, Savannah"?

"My auntie's dead," said Savannah. "And her husband killed her, and he's dead, too. He killed himself so the police wouldn't take him to jail. Now my cousins --"

Savannah could not complete her sentence. She was overtaken by grief once more, and this time Rosie cried. They both cried together and the storm grew stronger as the two woman rocked the love seat upon which they sat. Then Rosie said,

"Savannah, why are you here"?

"This is the most peaceful place I know," answered Savannah. "I did not know where else to go."

. "Surely, you can't work today, Savannah," said Rosie desperately, in an authoritative and motherly tone.

"I know," said Savannah, defensively. "I just wanted to -- He told her she would never get away from him. He told her it did not matter how many other women he had or how he treated her or how miserable she was, she would have to live with him for the rest of her life. Last week, Auntie got fed up. She moved in with my mother and my two sisters and me. Everything was going all right, it seemed. Auntie was free. She did not know what she would do in the long run, but she had some peace. She thought she did what was best for herself and her children.

"Yesterday, she was on her way to work, as usual. She stopped at the donut place at her usual time to get breakfast. When she walked out of the donut shop, and began to walk across the street, she saw a car coming straight at her. She probably saw that it was her husband before he ran her over. He kept running her over, back and forth, and he dragged her down the street with his car. When he was satisfied, he sped away with my auntie's blood still on the wheels. It was broad daylight. The police were right behind him. He fled to his house, and he retrieved the shotgun out of his bedroom. Then he went in the backyard and shot himself to death. My cousin was in the house when it happened."

There was not much to say after Savannah's recapitulation of the previous day's gruesome events. There was just loss, emptiness, abandonment, a hole, and two women clinging to one another, terrified, with no answers, scared half to death. As the children played, unscathed by the torture of Savannah's reality, safe in the security of comfort and hope in their dreams, another day dawned on Day Care Rafiki.

E^{leven}

THE GOSPEL
ACCORDING TO MARY

Savannah's family tragedy throbbed like a dull ache in Rosie's chest. She did not know Savannah's auntie or uncle or cousins, but she felt Savannah's pain. Savannah's pain was probably not as extreme as the pain of her cousins who lost their parents, but it was pain, indeed. Somehow, we are all connected to one another, and we will realize it once we feel the love between us.

Rosie loved Savannah like her own sister. What bothered Rosie the most about the death of the auntie is that she was killed on her path to freedom from the abuse her husband had inflicted upon her. Would Rosie's Bigmama have been killed had she decided to leave her husband? Would their divorce have been a worse tragedy than the pain of their marriage had been? What about Rosie's quest for freedom, her decisive move to leave and divorce Cookie? Would Rosie, too, be stopped dead in her tracks?

Rosie had so many questions, and she was uneasy. How could the pain of sin still touch her if the love of God was so all-consuming? She needed answers to difficult questions, and she believed she could only be comforted at the feet of the minister at Timothy's church. She had never heard anyone speak so eloquently and effectively to the questions that gnawed at her. Even though she had not become a member of Tim's church, she remembered the comfort she received from the ladies who consoled her after she first heard a message from Minister Beacon. She wanted to hear more of what made her heart cry out for joy and more of what made her reach beyond herself to touch the unseen.

~

The church was aglow with the joy of the congregation coming together for its weekly gathering. It was not as crowded today as it had been the first time Rosie attended, but it was just as warm and peaceful. Rosie thought to herself,

"This is going to be my home."

Rosie's children squirmed a bit in their seats, but for the most part they remained content with the coloring crayons and activity books Rosie brought for them to entertain themselves.

As the choir sang, so did Rosie's heart. Rosie had always liked music, and this music was special. There was something inspiring about many voices singing the same words together in harmony. They were dressed in blue and white choir robes, and the only thing one could see of each member were their hands and faces. They were all in one accord, like one creature with many faces and many hands, praising God. The music was rhythmic, and it was vibrant. The lyrics were pointed. They spoke to Rosie's longing. The choir sang:

"I'm glad to be in God's service. I'm glad to be in God's service. I'm glad to be in God's service, one more time. He didn't have to let me live. He didn't have to let me live. I'm glad to be in God's service one more time."

Rosie repeated to herself, "He didn't have to let me live." These specially charged words took root in her heart and germinated.

Minister Beacon began her sermon with greetings to the congregation like before, and she bowed her head to pray. Then she began.

~

"There was a strange stirring in the air," began the Minister. The woman saw a crowd moving purposefully and pointedly in an impassioned procession. She found herself pressed into the throng.

"'What is this,' she said aloud.

"'Where are we going,' she asked.

"'Why are we so angry?'

"In the throws of her bewilderment, her eyes were seized by the madness of this movement, the focal point of this fury, and she beheld He whom her soul loved. He was on a hill, and He was far from her reach. He was lifted up. He was nailed, feet and hands, to a rugged cross. Blood covered the body of her Beloved, the hands that had lifted her from the dregs of her wretchedness were cruelly impaled and stood fast to the cross, and His body quivered with pain.

"'His hands,' she uttered, 'His feet, oh, his sacred head.'

"As the crowd laughed at Him and taunted Him,

terror filled her heart. He hung His head and died.

"Darkness enshrouded the woman like an iron robe. They took her beloved away and laid Him in a tomb. Sorrow seized her. The earth moved beneath her. Her Beloved lay dead in a tomb. Never had a man loved her so dearly. Never had a man held her so near to himself. She could still feel the breath that came from his lips as He spoke the words that set her free,

"'Go and sin no more.'

"'How could -- why would -- how could they -- how could we do something like this,' she wailed.

"'He did no wrong,' she exclaimed.

"'He loved me. He touched me. He healed me. It was me. I am the one they wanted,' she wailed.

"But her cries were to no avail. Her beloved Savior lay motionless and enshrouded.

"'He loved me so much,' she wept.

"'He gave His life for me.'

"Her eyes were opened. She gazed over the corpse of her fruitless motions in this world through the eyes of her Savior. As she lay on the altar, a sacrifice unto the Most High Creator of heaven and earth, He circumcised her heart.

He cut away the shackles that held her bound, and He buried her in His death.

"Mary sought Him because her soul loved Him. Her life lay in that tomb. She was buried in His death and she would not go away. She could not go away. Even from the hold of the grave she was stayed, to be released only by the light of His presence. When she arrived at the tomb, the stone was removed, and her Master was not there. She had followed from the time He touched her, and now, not knowing where He was, she lamented.

"Two angels dressed in white heralded Him. She turned once and then again, and her Beloved stood before her very eyes. He surrounded her and embraced her in His spirit, yet she could not touch Him. Her heart leapt within her for joy. The sun shown brightly as she ran to tell the good news. 'He is risen! He is risen from the dead! And he ascends to his Father and your Father.' John 20:17

"He had risen! And He raised her up in His resurrection. She had confessed her sin to Him, and He took it upon himself. He was nailed to the cross to pay her debt. He freed her from the dead works which held her bound lifeless to the corpse of her damnation, and she arose from the tomb with her Beloved, her Liberator."

The minister paused for a moment and then looked at the congregation from over the tops of her horn-rimmed spectacles.

"That is the gospel according to Mary," she said.

"Each one of us has a gospel story to tell," she continued.

"We can tell of the good news of how Jesus set us free," she exclaimed, smiling broadly.

"God speaks the gospel to us personally."

"When God wants to set us free, He visits us in our various prisons, and from within our self-made and man-made prison cells, the Father calls us to be loosed from shackles. He calls us to a higher level of consciousness. He makes us aware of the operation of His Spirit if we would only live in the truth. That is what happened to Mary. She followed Jesus to the grave because she had become dead to the life she had lived before she met Christ.

"The plan of God for our lives is revealed to us in the light of the law, or standard of accepted behavior for God's people. That law is only comprehended in belief on the Savior who died in order to resurrect us from death, the

Savior who has the key to set us free.

"Keeping the law is often opposed to what we want to do, yet it is most effective for the soul exercised by such adversity to adhere to the law through the power of Christ. God's law is not the enemy. Keeping God's law is the process whereby we neutralize the jailer of our captivity, the jailer being the sin within us. Read Romans 7:20 when you get a chance. It is sin that opposes our every effort to become free.

"After Jesus comes with the key to unlock the prison and everything within it, the doors and the shackles and the bars on the windows, He sends the Holy Ghost with fire to transform and purify the soul which had been in prison. The Holy Ghost consumes all that is not like God, and the sinner becomes new by the burning of His fire. John the Baptist called it being baptized in fire. Jesus baptizes with fire and with the Holy Ghost, and through His baptism a soul may experience perfect love which casts out all fear.

"Your opportunity will not be to study a divine occurrence of this phenomenon in another person's life. Such a study is only familiarization unless it is mixed with the measure of faith from within the beholder. You may

read about Saul of Tarsus and his conversion and be
amazed. You may think on Stephen, the first martyr for
Jesus, and marvel. You may wonder after the works of
Abraham and proudly claim him as your father. You may
recall Anna, how she served the Lord with prayers and
fastings from the time of her early widowhood.

"You may think on Mary, the virgin, who was found
with child by the power of the Holy Ghost, or Elizabeth and
Sarah, those who had been barren and whose wombs had
been filled with the makings of those who would be mighty
men of God. Though many are called to serve, their service
cannot be imputed to others. Though many are baptized
into the water, this baptism experience cannot be imputed.
One can only be saved by being baptized for oneself, and in
repentance, actually stepping into the watery grave with the
intention of being buried with Christ and becoming a new
creature unto eternal life through Christ's resurrection.

"When the Lord, himself, comes to you through His
Spirit that He may baptize you in the fire, lay yourself down
on the altar of obedience to God's law and be consumed of
the fire of His anointing Holy Ghost in order to be purified
in His presence. Oh, that we may commune with Jesus, the

sacrificial Lamb in His sufferings, He that was slain from the foundation of the world for the purging of our sins. Then shall we be able to teach the anatomy of the believer. Then shall we be called disciples of the Most High God, and we shall be known by the angels which are from above."

~

"Over and over again," Rosie thought, "the theme of 'from death to life' keeps repeating itself. The death of Savannah's auntie, the death of Jesus Christ, Mary going to a dead man's grave, what was all this?" she thought. Rosie had accepted Christ's love, and she saw her soul's need for His love. But the death of Jesus, she did not quite comprehend. She wanted to live, not die. Yet Minister Beacon was now preaching that we should step into the "watery grave" and be "buried" in Christ's death. Rosie did not understand how death would bring her life.

As she pondered Minister Beacon's sermon at the end of the service, Rosie was startled by Tim's outstretched hand. "Hi, Rosie, he said." "I'm glad you could join us today."

As Rosie shook Tim's hand, he pulled her up to her feet and gave her a warm hug. He picked up Rosie's youngest daughter, Andrea, and her oldest daughter, Joy, drew closer to him. He said to Rosie,

"There's someone over here who wants to meet you."

Then he led her and her little flock to where Minister Beacon was standing. The Minister's arms were open wide and she smiled warmly as she cradled Rosie.

"Welcome, my child," she said. "Welcome home."

Rosie felt as though she had just won the jackpot. The minister who had just spoken to the whole congregation, who obviously had a personal connection with Jesus, called her, "my child."

"I *am* home," Rosie thought to herself. "I am home."

Minister Beacon invited Rosie and her children to her house for dinner, an invitation which Rosie graciously accepted.

Twelve

DINNER AT THE BEACONS'

Minister Beacon's house was warm and peaceful. She was a married woman. She had four children, all of whom were grown and living away from home. Minister Beacon's husband was a minister, too. They told Rosie to call them Ma and Pa Beacon. After a little talk and a drink of cool lemonade, Ma Beacon invited Rosie and her children to the table, where they partook of a simple yet satisfying meal.

There was something about the Beacons that made Rosie feel as though they were her family. The most apparent reason would be that they told her to call them Ma and Pa, but there was something more. They talked to Rosie about many things, her family, her upbringing, her marital status, her occupation and many other things. Rosie was not a bit shy and even welcomed the attention the Beacons lavished on her. But she was curious as to where all this talk was leading.

"Rosie," said Pa Beacon, sitting back in his chair, well content with the meal he had just eaten, "there is something in you that we seek to develop."

Rosie, not quite understanding how he could be interested in developing something in her, one he hardly knew, said, "Huh?" He repeated what he said.

"There is something in you that we seek to develop."

"Oh," said Rosie. Pa Beacon continued.

"It is our mission to employ people in the movement that leads from death to life, from blindness to sight and from sorrow to joy."

"What kind of people are these," thought Rosie. "What is he talking about? How can they make blind people see and dead people live"?

Since Pa Beacon brought it up, though, Rosie thought now would be a good time for her to find out how life comes from death. So she asked Ma Beacon about her sermon.

"You said in your sermon we must be buried in Jesus' death," started Rosie.

"What did you mean by that"?

"The message that you seek from God," answered Ma Beacon, "is one that will set you free. The message is that the death, resurrection and ascension of the human race is bound up in the Father's love for, the Son's passion for and the Holy Spirit's perpetual wooing of His people."

"I don't think I follow you," said Rosie.

"This is a simple message. The gospel is not complex. It speaks of life overcoming death. It speaks of slaves becoming free. It speaks of love as the single most liberating factor that a person can know."

"It doesn't sound like a simple message to me," thought Rosie.

"But I'm not a slave, and I'm not dead," she replied. "I'm just a little confused sometimes. I don't want to be lonely anymore. I don't want to be used anymore, and I don't want to do things that hurt me anymore. Nobody owns me, though. I make my own mistakes."

"And you will continue to make mistakes and hurt yourself and be used by others until you come to an understanding of what your life is about," replied Pa Beacon.

"Most of us have little understanding of the meaning of our lives," he continued.

"Though it is obvious to some people that a person is a small part of a big picture, we don't see the big picture. We usually see a person's life as a period of time that spans from birth to death. We wish to show you a broader perspective. Your life is bigger than the period between your physical birth and your physical death. We wish to invite you into the life of spirit, where time travel is possible, indeed imperative if you wish to live forever."

"Can people really live forever?" queried Rosie.

"Eternal life is a foreign reality to a person who believes her life exists between the two poles of birth and death," answered Pa Beacon, "but if your eyes were opened, you would see things as they are."

"Are you saying that I'm blind?" retorted Rosie.

"Only if you want to be," said Pa Beacon.

"The angels must cry as they watch the people of God struggling to crawl out from under the rock placed upon us, intended to entomb us," continued Ma Beacon.

"The enemy seeks to silence the voices which would sing the high praises of the Creator God. Mishandled and misinformed, many of God's people stumble in darkness as we seek the face of He who alone can set us free.

"You are fighting a battle against death. Someone is trying to destroy you. Your death, your blindness, and your slavery was initiated by Satan, and it is perpetuated by your ignorance. We have come to enlighten you."

Rosie wanted to leave just then. She was so embarrassed. It was as though she were naked before the Beacons. They saw her in the secret places. Why were they saying these words? They were so unconventional. It was as though they were trying to indoctrinate and hypnotize her at the same time. Rosie tried to leave, but the words that Ma and Pa Beacon spoke were so heavy, they weighed her down and would not allow her to speak or to move.

"It may appear that your enemy is on the outside of you," continued Ma Beacon, "but the most present danger in your life is misunderstanding the battle. It is not he who seeks to devour you that poses the greatest threat to your being. Rather, it is your entanglement in your own desires and self-deceit which neutralizes your ability to ward off the enemy.

"Our salvation depends on our belief in the Savior who fights the battle which is levied against us. He fights it for us and through us. We call Him the Savior, because He saves His people from their sins. He saves his people from the forces of evil which seek to annihilate us. We want you to see life as it is, and when you do see, we want you to tell others what you see."

Suddenly, Rosie began to feel the weight of responsibility upon her. She knew that the Beacons were presenting to her the answer from God which she sought in wrong places. He had come to fix her broken life, and God was speaking directly to her through His ministers, the Beacons.

She was humbled by His glory and complete care for her soul. She fell at the feet of the ministers and wept profusely. As Ma Beacon held her close, Pa Beacon put a Bible in Rosie's hands.

Thirteen

THE DEVIL GETS BUSY

As Rosie lay on the sofa bed in her small bedroom in the back of the house, she fell asleep with the overhead light beaming on her. She was awakened by a sound like that of flies buzzing directly into her ear. But her awakening was not to full consciousness. She was now in a semi-conscious, dream-like state. Her eyes being open and her body lying in the prone position, she felt her head being turned by a force outside of herself so that she was now lying upon her right ear whereas she had been lying upon her left ear before. She knew that a menacing and sinister spirit had invaded her sleep.

She began to call on the name of Jesus, but a force

from without herself prevented her vocal cords. So she thought on his name. Over and over again, she thought the name, "Jesus, Jesus, Jesus, Jesus ...," until she could feel the evil spirit being lifted, thereby allowing her to awaken fully. As she awoke, she fell upon her knees, quivering and praising God for saving her life. She knew she had been attacked by the devil in her sleep. She could not see him, and she could not touch him, but she felt him and she heard him, and he tried to stop her from calling on the name of Jesus. She discovered that the devil is powerful. She also discovered that the name of Jesus is greater than the devil. She meditated on Jesus' name, and the enemy fled.

The fact that the enemy constrained her vocal cords was amazing to Rosie. By this very act, she became aware that the enemy knows his plans are confounded and he is destroyed by the word of righteousness, the name of Jesus.. Though Rosie realized the power in the name of Jesus she spoke, she still feared. She located the Holy Bible that Pa Beacon had given her and she read it. She read it every night before she went to bed and placed it in arms reach of where she slept so that she could read it if ever the devil tried to accost her again. She had only one more similar encounter. Each time she felt as though fear or doubt or unseen forces would swallow her up, she read the Bible.

The conversation that Rosie had with the Beacons on the day before had gently interwoven itself with her heartbeat. She could not stop thinking about the things they had told her. She felt that if she could understand the mysterious code in which they seemed to be speaking, she would have a greater understanding of God's plan for her life. Before Rosie met the Beacons and became reacquainted with Tim, she had been undiscerning in her study into spirituality, but now she seemed to be having a conversation with God, somehow, that defied her reason.

She was now experiencing her search for the meaning of life with a new understanding. She wished to share and sound out this new revelation of God, and she shared her thoughts with her mother. Rosie's mother was a good sounding board but she did not have much to say about Rosie's religious experiences. She just wanted Rosie to be happy and good at whatever she did. Rosie's mother always told her,

"Be the best at what you choose to do. If you want to be a garbage collector, be the best garbage collector there is. And if you want to be a teacher, be the best teacher there is." Some parents Rosie knew went so far as to say, "If you want to be a whore, fine. Just be the best whore there is."

The tenet to which Rosie's mother held of being "the best" is nothing strange to children growing up in a competitive society. It is a coping mechanism and a tool of survival used in a world that shun people it deems to be losers. It is natural for a mother to push her child to be the best when she knows that her child's 100- percent effort may be worth only one quarter of a dollar in comparison to another mother's child who is given three dollars for her 25-percent effort.

As there are oftentimes bones of contention between mother and daughter, there were many disagreements and much misunderstanding between Rosie and her mother. The fundamental difference between Rosie and her mother was their vision of success. Rosie's mother wanted her to climb to the top of the proverbial ladder to success. Rosie wanted to climb Jacob's ladder spoken of in Genesis Chapter 28 instead. There was enmity between Rosie and her mother. It had been cultivated by the oppression and violation that they had both experienced in childhood, making it difficult for them to relate to one another.

One day, Rosie visited her mother. She told her how much she loved her and how lucky a person is to have a mother. They spent time talking about things, but not much time. Their conversations rarely went too deep, because if they did, they might end up in debate and then silence and then an awkward departure. They did understand, however, the need to maintain a relationship in spite of the pain it sometimes caused them. After all, they were mother and daughter. They belonged to one another.

When Rosie proceeded to leave her mother's house, her attention was diverted from her homeward aim to the steps of the next door neighbor's house. The weather was a bit chilly, and it was dark outside, yet two young women were sitting on the front steps. A scantily-clad toddler of about two sat in her stroller near the women. She did not even have on a jacket. The pungent odor of marijuana wafted in the air in the vicinity of the women and child.

Rosie wanted to continue on her way home, but she could not. She thought that if Tim were here he would have probably stopped to talk to these two women and "clear the air." Rosie wanted to be more like Tim. She wanted to break the wall that kept her from caring for and participating in the lives of the people around her.

. "They'll probably say I should mind my own business and maybe even curse me out, because they're probably high off that weed they're smoking," thought Rosie, "but I need to talk to them for the sake of the little girl."

Rosie opened the trunk of her car and pulled out a child's jacket.

"The jacket is a little big," she thought, "but it will do the job."

Rosie approached the two young women cautiously, praying that the Lord would give her words to say.

"Are you guys all right," queried Rosie.

"Yeah, we're fine," said one of the two women, thinking to resume her conversation with the other. Then Rosie said,

"Oh." After a brief pause she began again.

"I was just wondering why you're sitting outside in the cold and dark with that baby who isn't wearing a jacket."

There was silence, thick silence, as the young women tried to reason through the fog of their inebriation and give Rosie a sound answer. Eventually, Rosie broke the silence as she offered the jacket.

"I know it's a little big, but it will keep her warm," said Rosie; "you can keep it."

The women were surprisingly grateful for the intrusion, especially the mother of the little girl. The other woman politely excused herself and left. Rosie talked with the mother of the child for some time. The woman expressed to Rosie that she was having trouble getting along with her auntie at home, and that is why she was out here talking with a friend in the cold.

She confided in Rosie that she was living with her auntie because her mother had died. She said that she had been lying in the bed with her mother one night when her mother gave her lasting words of encouragement. Shortly thereafter, an aneurism burst in her mother's head and she died with her daughter lying there by her side.

The young woman opened up to Rosie as though she was just waiting there for someone to talk to, someone with whom she could share the blessing of encouragement and faith. Rosie talked to the young woman about Jesus and the power He shares with all who find Him and cling onto Him, and they prayed. Then they parted company, both of them heading home.

When Rosie arrived, it was late at night. Apparently, Timothy had come by her apartment that evening, and he left her a message, a sad, sad message. His mother had been shot to death that very day, and she died in his arms. Rosie was stunned with disbelief.

"How could someone just shoot somebody's mother like that," she thought. "How can Tim bear the hurt he must be feeling right now."

She went out in the night trying to find him, to tell him that she was there if he needed her, but she was only able to leave a message with his brother-in-law. She felt so helpless. She could only pray for healing. She could only fall on her knees and into the arms of God. She had no answers, but one thing was evident. The devil does get busy.

Fourteen

THE FUNERAL

The funeral held in the memory of Tim's mother was attended by many people. It was hard for Rosie to comprehend how a Christian woman could die such a death. That is how the crack addicted and some prostitutes and even some babies born to irresponsible parents die, but not Christians, she thought. That is how victims of robbery and rape die, but not Christian mothers. The ghetto streets are where the reckless IV drug users, homosexual males and illicit sex participants die of AIDS, but not Christian mothers. Something had gone seriously wrong here. How could it have happened? The war that was fought on the ghetto streets between the gangsters and the other gangsters and between the cops and the gangsters was coming closer to home.

Many people stood up and spoke of the goodness of Tim's mother, and the people cried. Some sang. Tim walked up to the front of the church, braced himself with the help of a couple of strong men and sang in honor of his mother and the victory in Jesus. Her children and grandchildren cried. Then it was over.

The pallbearers carried the coffin, and the people filed out of the church. Then there was a new beginning. Now, a family would be forced to live with the reality of its mother being violently torn far away from its embrace. Now, some of those who had been blind before would see that violent death is an equal opportunity employer. It comes not only to the violent and criminal and diabolical haters of God, but it comes to God's people, too.

Rosie had come to know that she was not the only one seeking deliverance from the afflictions she suffered, but there were many who sought God's healing. Many came to Him with their wounds, seeking that He would make them whole. Many others drifted aimlessly in the cesspools of their afflictions on the battlefield of life. They were casualties of a war they did not even suspect was taking place. Women, men and children were dying spiritually, mentally and physically all around Rosie as the war of ages raged.

Though Rosie did not know Timothy's family and friends before the funeral, she became acquainted with them as they all drew closer together for prayer and Bible study to fill a precious space left by their mother. When they gathered together, they traveled to different homes. They sang, they cried, they prayed and they shared their thoughts and feelings about things. What Rosie found very intriguing about the gatherings was the teaching and exposition of the Bible that was the highlight of each meeting. Sometimes they debated and were very serious. Sometimes they played games and laughed, still being serious. Yet they desired always to redeem the time against the wickedness of the age. They lifted up the word of God to be shone in its positive light.

One evening, after the sun had set on a Sabbath day, ushering in a new week, Rosie and her new friends found themselves down by the river. It was a cool evening, and a silver streak from the full moon shone majestically on the water. They were playing a game similar to charades. The difference was that they did not act out a character in silent pantomime form, but they described the character with much detail, the details being a Bible story.

Kathy stood up and said,

"Guess who I am." She then proceeded to describe the character she sought to portray.

"I shudder to think of the iniquity that has been wrought through me, one who was chosen to be a vessel of God's honor. Reminiscing on my past is like watching a cliff-hanger movie. I close my eyes and shudder sometimes when I think back over my life. I am like a beautiful flower that grows from dirty mud.

"I am as weak as a bag of blood which could be burst by the blast of rapid fire, yet the awful scourge of universal evil is subject to obliteration through the life of He who is the fruit of my womb. My enemy is Satan and he oftentimes has worked his evil through me. I have come over a rocky way, and my burden is heavy. I am traveling to a land called Zion, and I trust in God.

"For though the heavens fall, though I be desecrated, raped, pillaged and destroyed, though my heart cry out for my children as the dragon proceeds to destroy them, we shall endure this war and we shall be victorious.

"My life is as the birthing of a stubborn child. There are times of labor, and there are times of rest. Sometimes I see past blue skies to the throne of God, and sometimes I am delirious and hell-bent.

"If you were to attempt to see me in my fullness, you would hardly see me at all. You may even testify that I do not exist. You would be as one blind man spoken of in an Indian proverb who touched the tail of an elephant and described the elephant as a snake or another blind man that touched the legs of the elephant and described it as a tree. I am the whole of the elephant and much more.

"Did anybody guess yet?" queried Kathy. A resounding, "No" echoed through the group. They wanted to hear more. So Kathy continued.

"I will come closer to you so you can see me. I will place myself in this story so you can know me. Listen closely, discern fully. Be fearful and tremble. Hear the word of the Lord.

"The human race has now fallen into a sinful state of separation from God, yet it was not that way in the beginning. When God first created us, He planned that we should be safe from all hurt, harm and danger. So He created a safe place in which we would live from the beginning of the world. I am the woman that was in the Garden, and this is how it began."

"I know," blurted out Juan, "You're Eve."

"Sorry," said Kathy with a big grin, "that's not quite the answer I'm looking for. Now, can I finish my story"?

"But there was only one woman in the garden," said Juan.

"Oh, really?" questioned Kathy.

"Just go ahead," shouted one.

"By all means," stated another.

"You go girl," encouraged somebody else. Kathy continued.

"The Lord God made a surrounding protection about us. It was like a fence. We call it the garden. God then placed the garden eastward in Eden. Eastward means ancient or beginning. Eden was a delightful, pleasurable and delicate place. Just think of your fairest and purest imaginations of paradise. Eden was that and much, much more. In the beginning, God wanted to protect us in Eden so we could show off His glory.

"We shined as a light in the earth, and we shined throughout the universe from the earth as we were pleased to dwell in God. The devil saw our light, and the devil saw our love for one another and our love for God, and he could not stand it. He burned with jealously. Eventually, there was war, the magnitude of which is not, was not, cannot be, nor will ever be equaled. The furies of the evil one were aimed directly at me as the serpent sought to gain an entry into the heart of the man and the woman God had created.

"There is no mistake about it. We disobeyed. But because the advantage the serpent took over us was so great, it took me a long time to admit my wrong. We were forced out of Eden and out of the garden. It seemed a harsh penalty to pay for eating the forbidden fruit, and I wanted God to know it was the serpent's fault, not mine. I mean, you look at it. Can you imagine being forced out of paradise and into the desert wilderness? Can you imagine the God of the universe banishing you from His presence?

"We suffered indescribable pain. The man who had been so devoted to his wife now blamed the woman for our woes. Perhaps he thought that if he delivered her up to God, he would get some kind of reward for his feeble attempt to save himself. Maybe he thought God would kick her out of the Garden and save him. Huh, the man and the woman were made for each other, and they suffered together. Marriage is not always a bed of roses, and we were facing the heat of hell. Because of our disobedience to God's word, that we should not eat of the fruit of the tree of the knowledge of good and evil, the seed of sin had been planted in our hearts, and the fruit of death would be our reward.

"We were driven out of the garden of our paradise and left with no protection. We could not go back into the garden, because Cherubim were placed right at the front door of it. We could not live eternally, because a blaze covered the tree of life with drought and destruction in the form of a flaming sword.

"Now that we had fallen into disobedience, we were no longer in our safe, high station in the garden of God. The land was not pleasant anymore. It was cursed for Adam's sake. Besides that, the devil, who had enticed us into sin, sought to entice us into eternal damnation through the destruction of our eternal souls. If he could cause us to curse God and refuse the salvation He would offer us from this wilderness, the devil would have won what would amount to a hollow victory for him, yet it would be death certain to us. Rebelliousness against God is iniquity. Iniquity is a mystery into which misguided and foolish souls are inducted. There is no reason for rebelliousness, and it yields only the fruit of death.

"Upon evicting us from the garden, Yahweh gave us hope and a rough way to travel as He began to reveal to us the new home which He had prepared for us, the ark of His covenant. Now, we would learn to dwell in the Word of God. All else was vain. The land we inherited brought forth thorn and thistle. We would eat bread from it 'in the sweat of the man's face.' There was no inherent joy in childbirth. It was as sorrow multiplied for the woman. But Yahweh gave us a dwelling place in His Word.

"It was an awful edict and it would require a bloody war. From the midst of the blood bath would spring forth our life and eternal abode. In the Word of God was placed the key that would unlock the door granting us passage from the death we had bought with our sins to the eternal life Yahweh bought for us in the blood of the Lamb. This is the word within which mankind finds safety and the devil finds destruction:

"'And I will put enmity between thee and the woman, and between thy seed and her seed; it shall bruise thy head, and thou shalt bruise his heel.' (Genesis 3:15)

"It was the word of prophecy that we would live within, the word of prophecy being safety indeed. Because of the state of the flesh, we had become enslaved. Satan had become our master because the sin-cursed earth had become Satan's kingdom. Yet because Yahweh had given us the gift of the will, He would be able to restore us to the state of bliss and joy if we desired to return to Him. Through our belief in the word of God, a path would be illumined amidst the darkness of Satan's kingdom, guiding us back to the garden, and then Satan, along with his evil angels and the sin-cursed earth together with any of our children who refused to walk in the light, would be destroyed.

"The word of prophecy is simply Yahweh communicating with His people. As He issued the curse against the serpent in the garden, He was preparing a dwelling place for us. The seed or child that I would bear would utterly destroy the serpent, or bruise his head, and the serpent would kill my seed, the Savior of humanity, the one who would rise from the hold of the grave with the keys of death and hell in His hand. The word of this prophecy gives hope to the people who choose to believe in Yahweh and His promises. It is a light that shines on a path that leads the believers through many generations until the prophecy shall be fulfilled.

"Though I, as Eve, thought I would bear the savior, I did not; nor did any of my daughters, granddaughters or great granddaughters.

"Hey," protested Juan, "you said you're not Eve."

"Eve is not totally me," retorted Kathy, "but I am some Eve. Now, can I finish my story"?

"Yeah, go ahead," said Juan, somewhat perplexed.

"Carry on, my sister," said another.

"You just tell it like it is," said somebody else. Kathy continued.

"The child which fulfilled the prophecy that was first given at the beginning of creation, which would utterly destroy the serpent which enticed the earth into sin, was not born until many generations after the prophecy of the woman's seed was given. Yet it was a light that the believers nurtured, the candlestick which we kept burning that led us until the prophecy should be fulfilled.

"Through the word of prophecy, we are able to see beyond the veil of Satan's kingdom into the holy places where the people of Yahweh are walking. We travel through a bloody path of tears and woes, and in the midst of it all, the devil, his converts and his power is being destroyed. Beyond the veil of Satan's illusory kingdom, which casts strange light and falsehood in order to prevent God's people from becoming free in His sanctuary, is revealed the abominableness of Satan's kingdom and the glory of the Kingdom of God.

"Confusion has come upon the earth because of sin. The devil deceived us into believing that God is as Satan is. He misrepresented God in our eyes, and he was allowed to do so because of our desire to justify ourselves and stay in Eden. We would have to admit our wrong if we were to return to God. We would be required to travel through generations in order to be renewed and redeemed and restored.

"Now," said Kathy, looking around at the many sets of anticipating eyes, "who am I"?

"Whoa," said Darrell, "I know exactly who you are. But first let me say this, that recitation of prophecy was good. You just preach it, preacher," he exclaimed.

"Amen," said another one.

"Tell it, Sister," said yet another. Then Darrell continued,

"You are the church of the Living God."

"You're absolutely right," exclaimed Kathy.

"Yeah," shouted Darrell. And he continued.

"'Therefore rejoice, ye heavens, and ye that dwell in them. Woe to the inhabiters of the earth and of the sea! for the devil is come down unto you, having great wrath, because he knows that he has but a short time.'
(Revelation 12:12)

"Hallelujah," shouted Kathy.

"Praise God," exclaimed Juan.

The group marveled at the wonders of the Word of God. The air had grown a bit cooler. The group sat in silence, as if it had been contented by the dynamic of the story of the church in the wilderness. Kathy began to sing a song.

"Sweet hour of prayer," she whispered in a melodic

soprano voice, "Sweet hour of prayer." Everyone joined her in time, Rosie being the last, as she was still learning the song.

"If this is a club," thought Rosie, "I want to join.

"If it's a ship, I want to ride."

The group of worshipers, very exhausted at this time, closed its study in prayer, and they walked toward their cars on the way to their several dwellings. Some wept. Some shouted praises to God. Some sang. They bore the weight of the gospel in their bosom as they headed to a future free from the fetters of this world. They were as a motley, war-torn platoon of pilgrims pushing forward from yesterday's defeat to tomorrow's victory.

There was such compelling wonder in the fellowship of the people at Tim's church. Rosie was learning. She was growing. She had come to realize her potential. She had become part of a community with purpose, and at her next opportunity, Rosie was baptized and became a full-fledged church member.

F ifteen

AROUND THE LAKE

R osie awoke to a day overcast with clouds. As she rubbed the sleep out of her eyes, she fell on her knees and worshiped God. Preparing to take a walk and meditate on words of importance, like salvation and power and honor to God and abiding strength which transcends the weakness of flesh and topics of that vein, she embarked on a trip to Lake Merritt, the three-and-a-half-mile course for joggers and walkers and skaters and bikers and the like.

Rosie and her children got into her little green car and drove toward the lake. As they rounded the corner onto the street where customarily many illegal and shady deals took place, a heavy-set prostitute lifted her t-shirt to reveal two breasts, each of which was roughly the size and shape of a five-pound sack of potatoes. Rosie thought to herself,

"She probably did not expect us."

But then again, maybe she did not care who saw her. All she wanted was the money her body could buy. If Rosie showed the woman enough money, anything could have happened.

The city streets were infested with lost people who were too blind to find their way to straight paths. The broken liquor bottles and used IV needles and doorways which smelled of urine and the toothless smirks on the faces of people who continually hoped for less was the paint sprayed on the muraled walls of Rosie's community. Let alone the fact that many of these people were victims of poverty that was meted out against them by the able rich before they were born and before they had an opportunity to act in their own best interest, they had sold themselves to ignorance. Now they lived in the muck and mire that they spewed out of their own mouths, words that foretold their stagnation.

After she parked her car in a space overlooking the west end of the Lake, Rosie began her walk, her children running and giggling not too far ahead of her. The early morning breeze brushed across Rosie's cheeks as she walked around the lake. She thought of what Ma Beacon had told her about being baptized into the death of Jesus. It was an initiation of sorts. She thought about her own baptism. Baptism in the water and the communion with Christ in her inner self had separated her from the miasma of lifeless living that was taking place all around her. At the same time, it had equipped her to be a rescue worker in the salvation of the people who were perishing in her very midst.

As she continued to walk, men and women with taut bodies passed her by, the olympiads of their day. The high-rised apartments, Mercedes Benzes and the designer fashions were the decoration that laced the lake area, the heart of the city. Rosie saw an ex-governor who had also been a candidate for the presidential seat of the United States walking and jogging around the lake. She even met the mayor of the city near the lake. Despite the affluence of the area, Rosie sensed the desperation of the mad chase. Around and around the lake it went. As the serpent which chases its own tail and as the recycling of vain thoughts and hopes and ambitions, so was the life of the city, going around and around.

. To her left, a man, whose clothing it appeared had not been changed for over a year, rummaged through a trash receptacle. He found a half eaten bagel with cream cheese to eat, a pizza box to place over his head to shelter him from the rain and a pair of mismatched socks with holes in them to place on his hands or feet, whichever he chose.

To Rosie's right, ran a shapely, hard-bodied woman wearing a hot-pink, spandex tank top and biker pants to match. Her feet were clad with expensive, designer running shoes and gold chains swung around her neck. Diamonds studs were set in her ears, and rings with dangling things were on all of her fingers. Close behind her followed a man; he was well fit and handsome. Beads of sweat rolled from his forehead and arm pits and back and chest as he followed behind the woman in pink, tongue wagging, saliva dripping. He would follow and pass her, and she would follow and pass him. They continued on in this manner until they had chased one another out of Rosie's view.

As she continued to walk, Rosie saw a woman crying. Her lipstick was smeared. Her dress was torn, and her hair was disheveled. Then Rosie saw an angry man. He said to the woman,

"Shut-up, bitch, or I'll hit you again."

Nearby, a little girl sat motionless on a swing in the sandbox over-looking a little island on the lake. The island was designed to be a sanctuary for birds.

Rosie and her children completed their course around the lake. The children played a little while at Lakeside Park; then they got in the car and drove towards home. When Rosie stopped the car in front of her apartment, the children ran chasing one another to the front door and disappeared into the house before their mother could issue a word of protest. Rosie paused in the car to gather an armful of her belongings, and she witnessed two little children, a boy and a girl, being terrorized by an older woman near her vehicle.

The woman was angrily shouting and cursing at the little girl. From the vantage point of the little girl, the woman was big, and she was angry. The little girl was scared. The woman had a quick tongue. She could probably convince a flea to jump off of a dog with her words alone if she wanted to. Rosie really did not want to have any dealings with her, but the little girl was so helpless, so scared, so dejected. Rosie sat in the car trying to think about what she could do to help in this situation. While she sat, a man coming in their direction looked at the scene between the woman and the girl, looked at Rosie, laughed and walked across the street. Evidently, he did not even want to walk on the same side of the street where the angry woman and the frightened children stood. Putting the belongings that she had gathered down on the seat, Rosie got out of her car.

Rosie recalled the woman saying that because some people had stolen her money, she did not even have any money to buy food. That is where Rosie saw that she could make an entryway. She said to herself that she would offer the woman food and that would divert the woman's attention from the frightened little girl. Rosie found out that the woman was the grandmother of these two children.

When Rosie offered the woman assistance, the woman immediately took offense. Many times during the course of their conversation, the woman asked Rosie her age. Rosie, this young woman, was now butting into her business, and she felt like she was in the hot seat. Of course, one could say that if the grandmother had not have put her "business in the streets," no one would have known it and could not have butted in. Nevertheless, in this case, the woman's explosive behavior in plain view of all passers by was providential. It lent itself to mediation and correction and redemption.

As the brunt of the grandmother's anger was now being directed at Rosie, the little girl received immediate relief. Rosie pulled her close to herself and caressed her head and back. She rubbed her hands and squeezed her and rocked and cradled her. The woman saw what was happening, but she could not stop it.

Rosie's children saw their mother from the livingroom window. Wondering what was taking her so long to come in the house, they ran to meet her at the gate. Rosie instructed them to bring two apples for the two children and two children's Bible story books for them to read. The woman said that she did not take hand-outs and that she could not take any of Rosie's charity. Then Rosie proceeded to tell her of all the many handouts she was in possession of, like all the clothes on her back, the car she was driving and the shoes on her feet.

Though the woman had been very angry, her anger could not penetrate the invisible shield that surrounded Rosie and the little girl that was now in her embrace. Through Rosie's tender prodding, she was able to gather from the woman that she had been threatened by the visitors in her house at which time she fled, leaving her granddaughter, the little girl, in the house. The granddaughter was scared, so she ran out after her grandmother. The house being thus abandoned, the visitors stole the grandmother's money from inside of it. The grandmother contended that those people who had threatened her would not have hurt the child.

The older woman eased from her defensive position and began to trust Rosie a bit. The children graciously fed on the big red apples given them by Rosie's children and began looking at the pictures in the Bible books.

The grandmother said that she was raising her grandchildren because her daughter was addicted to crack cocaine and had lost control of her life. It became apparent to Rosie that the grandmother was a crack addict, also. The grandmother further revealed to Rosie that she was abused by her husband. The family was in utter need. Rosie must have talked with the grandmother on that corner for about two hours. Rosie told her about the salvation of Jesus, and assuring her that she could steal away to Jesus, revealed to her that He was her hope.

Rosie invited the woman and her grandchildren to church for prayer meeting. The woman said she did not have any clothes to wear. Rosie told her she would give her clothes. The woman said she did not take charity. Rosie invited the woman inside of her house for a meal. The woman declined to accept the invitation.

The grandmother was much calmer when she left with her grandchildren by her side, but what she had to look forward to, God only knows. The children, much happier now, swung their new Bible books by their sides and licked their apple sweet lips.

Sixteen

THE FALL

Rosie had come home particularly tired after a long day of work at the day care. Her children were running back and forth through the house as she lay on her bed. She would soon get up and prepare the evening meal. The telephone rang and after having answered it, Rosie's daughter, Joy, called out to her,

"Mom, Ma Beacon's on the phone."

Rosie was a bit groggy as she awakened from what had turned out to be a five-minute power nap, contrary to her best intentions to take a "real" nap.

"Hello, Ma Beacon, said Rosie, "It's good to hear your voice."

"Mm-hmm. Mm-hmm.

"Yes, I had a good day. We went on a field trip. We took the children for pony rides."

Andrea and Joy looked on intently, listening to their mother's one side of the two-way conversation she held over the telephone. Joy whispered something to Andrea and they both giggled.

"Yes, ma'am.

"A week of prayer?"

"Really? You want me to speak?

"I can do that," said Rosie, as a rush of adrenaline flowed through her body.

"Yes, ma'am.

"Yes, ma'am.

"Thank you, Ma Beacon. I'll be there. I won't let you down."

Rosie hung up the phone and assumed her evening duties. She cooked, fed the children and got them bathed and in the bed. Then she began to study the Bible and prepare her message. The church would hold a week of prayer and revival, and she would be one of the speakers. Rosie felt a great honor and responsibility had been placed upon her.

When the evening arrived that Rosie was slated to speak, her message was prepared. As she thought about what she would wear, she decided that her clothing should be modest, not calling much attention to herself, but beautiful, as she is a child of the Most High God. She covered her head with a nice hat. She meticulously placed her Bible and her notes in a book bag and placed it right by the door so she would not forget it. She made sure her children were dressed neatly and that their faces shined and that the strands of their hair were in reasonable proximity to "in place."

~

There was a nice crowd at the church, about 40 people. After closing her eyes and praying audibly before the congregation, Rosie began her message.

"Unholy desire is like a cancer which eats away at the mind and distracts from all pure endeavor," she began. "It is better for one to be content with what one has than to dwell in desire.

"Take TV, for instance. On the commercials we see pizza, cakes, fried chicken, hamburgers, sexy women and men, money, houses, cars, fame, fortune and all kinds of things that make us desire and leave us in want. We become discontent many times because we do not get what we want. Sometimes we get what we want, and it leaves us wanting more.

"There can be a battle in the mind in simply watching a television program. I know full well that when I watch TV, there is a great chance that I might experience internal struggle as I try to keep my mind on holy principles. Nevertheless, in an attempt to cool my brain down from meditating on very weighty themes, I occasionally brave the risk of television viewing. Sometimes I just want to sit and laugh, put my mind on automatic pilot and let my eyes glaze over.

"One evening I was feeling especially brave. I watched a show aired by a station that hits hard against a person's ability to keep her desires pure. It probably studies the human brain in an attempt to provoke it to lust. I yielded to temptation and viewed something I knew would stick in my psyche and possibly cause me to sin.

"Nevertheless, there was something interesting that I saw as I turned to that station this particular night. I watched a battalion of army men looking beyond some sort of invisible wall upon a scene which appeared very serene. On the other side of the invisible wall were what the army men called 'prairie people'. They depicted a time and place in America when pioneers rode from the east to the west in covered wagons in order to settle in the western territories. The women wore the long dresses and aprons, their hair flowing in the wind, flowers growing.

"The children played as though there was not a care in the world. The husband gazed lovingly at his wife, and the grandmother appeared as a symbol of stability and wisdom. To the army men on the outside of the invisible wall, all appeared well. But life beyond the wall showed a time in the past, and the wall was invisible. Logic told them that something was wrong.

"Enters an army man who was given the mission to find a way beyond the invisible wall. Let's just call him GI Getter. He was told that though the scene looked very benign, it might be dangerous for any of them to cross over to the other side. In an effort to accomplish his mission, GI Getter asked permission from his superior officer to use special equipment to listen to what the prairie people were saying. Such permission was denied.

"After much investigation and many attempts at breaking through the invisible wall, GI Getter found a way to get beyond it, though he did not reveal to anyone that he had accomplished his goal. As he observed the prairie people, he became fascinated with a young woman on the other side. He gawked at her so much that he began to desire her. Though he was denied permission to use special listening equipment, he did so anyway. When his commanding officer found that he had disobeyed his order in this particular, he took GI Getter off of the mission.

"As GI Getter sat under a tree under guarded custody, he had a plain view through the invisible wall. He gazed at the prairie woman, and his desire to touch her grew stronger. His desire got the better of him. At the time he had previously calculated that the invisible wall would be penetrable, he began to run towards it. Though his comrades attempted to stop him, he penetrated the invisible wall and landed beyond it. He was now in the land of the prairie people.

"As I stared at the television set, I knew something was getting ready to happen, and I did not want to see it, because I knew it was going to be bad. So I turned the channel with the remote control. But I just had to see what happened, so I turned it right back. The prairie woman looked a bit startled when the army man penetrated the invisible wall. She turned a bit, coyly smiling, as she looked down, the wind blowing her blond hair across her face. Then she went close to him, and he drew closer to her. She turned her face a bit, still smiling, and when she turned back towards him, she had sharp teeth as the teeth of a flesh-eating dinosaur.

I quickly turned the channel again with the remote control, because I did not want to see what was going to happen next. But it was pretty obvious what GI Getter's fate was. My curiosity got the better of me, and I turned back to the program I had been watching to witness all of the prairie people kneeling over GI Getter's body, devouring him; even the little boy and the little girl were feasting on his raw flesh. GI Getter's comrades looked on with horror and amazement from the safe side of the invisible wall. Fortunately for them, they now knew better than to come in close proximity with those prairie people.

"Had GI Getter listened to and obeyed his superior

officer, the chances are very good that he would not have died the tortuous death that he died. There are no guarantees in science fiction. But in the realm of reality, obedience to God does guarantee eternal life. There are many tools used by the enemy to intensify one's desire. If we are to get the better of the desire we are to distrust self and submit totally to the will of God in our lives.

"Dwelling on desire is living in the flesh. Living in the flesh does not mean living in the body, or the anatomy of the body. We all live there unless we are dead. Living in the flesh is dwelling in the state of want or desire as opposed to dwelling in the abundance of life offered by God. When we dwell in the flesh, we act according to the desire of our five senses, the senses of taste, touch, sound, smell and sight.

"The mind that is of the flesh will deceive the soul to the point of everlasting death, as is the nature of the flesh to do, as was the case of the fictional character GI Getter. Victory over the flesh is obtained as we breathe out our unworthiness in confession and breathe in the Spirit of God through his grace and mercy. If we let His Word live in our minds through the righteousness imputed to us by the blood of Jesus, we shall dwell on the safe side of desire.

"Confession takes place in the soul when we identify and admit malignity in our desires as tried against an unparalleled standard, the Holy Bible. A battle in the mind caused by the light which shines therein through the gospel indicates darkness or planned iniquity, fueled by unholy desire. The light of the truth in God's Word enters the mind and soothes as a healing balm when we truly believe it. Disharmony between the Word of God and the mind results when we covet pleasure in our own desire unsanctified by the light of God's desire for us.

"The soul is a vessel capable of being indwelt by spirit. 'God is a Spirit, and they that worship Him must worship Him in spirit and in truth.' John 4:23.

"And the enemy is a spirit, 'for we wrestle not against flesh and blood but against principalities, against powers, against the rulers of the darkness of this world, against spiritual wickedness in high places.' See Ephesians 6:12. High places are in our minds, situated at the tops of our bodies in our brains.

"So the soul, which is a vessel, becomes a battlefield for a great war between Christ and Satan. Many who may be content to live in Christ fail to discern between good and evil spirits and allow the spirit of unholy desire to dwell in them. The Lord would not have us ignorant concerning this battle for our loyalty to the cause of our spiritual survival.

"When the evil in this world came to be, taking its occasion to dwell in the hearts of men, so entered the devil's kingdom. Man doubts the word of God, that He is omnipotent. The commandments are life, and the war rages within human hearts. To the detriment of the evil and to the uplifting of a man's soul, God swore an oath that He would save by the blood of the Lamb of God, all that would enter into a covenant with Him.

"'For this is the covenant that I will make with the house of Israel after those days, saith the Lord; I will put my laws into their minds and write them in their hearts: And I will be to them a God, and they shall be to me a people.' Hebrews 8:10

"God's grace and mercy is the lighthouse standing in the middle of the stormy seas of our lives. It is the solitary, invincible cave in the midst of the battle ground of our fiery passions. We must relate to Him according to His Word. To be safe, we must worship Him according to His desire for our lives and not our words nor our desires for ourselves. The battle rages in the hearts of God's people, because without the souls of God's people, the devil has no kingdom. Yet God's love is so great that He gave His only begotten son, that whoever believes in Him should not perish but have everlasting life. John 3:16

"Desire in our hearts indicates need. We are needy because sin has robbed and has eroded our lives. Because a man may have stolen my brother's car, he is needy. Because I may have coveted my neighbor's house on the hill, I am needy. Because an early grave may have stolen my sister's husband, she is needy. Sin is like pollen that fills the air. It is not discriminating.

"The enemy inspired sin in rebelliousness. Because of his unhappiness, he seeks to upset the order of God's kingdom. As a vengeful adversary would kill a man's wife to break the man, so does the devil seek to destroy the apple of God's eye, His church.

"We must employ the wisdom of the Ancient of Days and speak out our unworthiness to abide this battle. If we come to the Creator with a broken and contrite spirit, entering into a covenant with God, we will survive all ill-intent. As this battle rages, let us hold firm to the winning army, the God army. Let us clothe our minds with truth, knowing that the battle is fought in our minds and through our actions. Let us desire this one thing, that we may be what God wants us to be."

~

Then Rosie sat down, and the congregation said, "Amen." Rosie was confident that she had communicated the Spirit's words to the people.

Throughout the delivery of her message, Rosie noticed a young man who was a member of the church. He was a very nice person. Though he held no official title, when the congregation met, he was often there to offer his assistance in tasks such as setting up chairs, cleaning up after pot luck meals and holding small children. Rosie found it a bit odd, though, that during her message he sat in the balcony all alone. He smiled at Rosie and made her feel sort of nice. His name was Larry.

As time went on, Larry paid more and more attention to Rosie. He was very playful, and her children liked him. Sometimes he would take Rosie and her children to different churches and to the park and to Lake Merritt and different places where he made them all feel so special. It appeared to Rosie that love was blooming.

One morning Rosie woke up at the crack of dawn. She and Larry planned to meet and watch the sun rise at a nature reserve area before going to church. With part of her mind, Rosie believed that this man could soon be her husband and that this courtship that was coming alive would bear the fruit of peace and happiness.

But there was a fear in the pit of her stomach, a feeling that was undeniable that something was just not right and that caution in dealing with him would be the better part of wisdom. Eventually, her passion got the better of Rosie, and she threw caution to the wind.

S eventeen

THE EMBRACE

R osie was transformed from a woman who went about with much power in the knowledge of her salvation to a weak, broken and tortured person. She barely made it through each day. As she was duty-bound to support herself and her children, she did go to work, but getting out of bed was a chore. She felt so used, so let down, so sinful, so deceitful. Larry was tall, dark and handsome. He had been raised in the church all of his life. He was a single man of means and potential. But he was a player, a smooth operator, a snake in the grass, and he seduced Rosie.

She felt as though she were starting over again, right from the beginning, like when she first came to know Jesus.

But it was worse this time. She had claimed to be a Christian before her sin this time. She had been baptized. She could not forgive herself, and she did not believe God could forgive her either. Before she knew Larry, Rosie faced the mornings with a smile. She sang and danced, and she was joyful. It seemed that all was bright and beautiful. After she knew Larry, she saw that she had sold her self cheap.

Rosie's children were feeling her pain. Though she tried to keep smiling and being joyful with them for their sakes, she could not do it alone. She needed to be lifted up.

One day as Rosie was going through her painful motions of simply living, there was a knock on the door. Rosie's daughter, Andrea, answered it. She squealed with delight when she saw Savannah standing on the other side of the door with lots of bags in her hand.

"Auntie Savannah," she hollered.

Then her sister came running.

"Auntie Savannah. Auntie Savannah."

"Is that all you see," shouted Roger; "we're here, too."

Savannah's son and daughter, Roger and Kim, filed

in close behind her. It was like a mini family reunion for the children.

There was something about Savannah. She could scratch just where it itched. She could bring a smile where before there was only pain. She was a grown woman herself, but she was like a child, in a sense. She had a way of bringing out the laughter in others, and she always knew how to get to Rosie.

Savannah put her bags on the table and pulled out five mangos. She gave one to each of the children. Then she removed five plates from the cabinet. She sliced each child's mango and laid it on a plate which she sat before each of them. Then she and Rosie went into the livingroom.

"I failed Him," said Rosie, breaking down in loud sobs.

Savannah held Rosie in a loving embrace. For a while, she said nothing. Savannah just rocked her and cradled her like Rosie was her own child.

"It's called repentance, Rosie," said Savannah.

"God knew the devil would try to separate you from Him, but he can not. God cares. He loves you, Rosie, no matter what you have done. You always have a place with

Him. Jesus is your Savior. Jesus is your friend. Don't just sit there; get back up."

Savannah touched Rosie beyond the feeling of her regret. She showed Rosie the tenderest of love. Though Rosie did not realize it then, she soon learned that if her sister, Savannah, could love her even in her sinfulness, God still loved her. Then Savannah turned on the music. She selected a tune from a male vocal group called Chosen. The words go something like this:

"You are my friend; you are my joy; you are my comforter, everything I desire. When I feel sad and lonely, you are the first on my mind." Jesus is the friend and comforter they were singing about. The words of the music and the beat brought a smile to Rosie's face she just could not wipe off. And they danced. Rosie and Savannah and the children danced.

E ighteen

THE MARRIAGE FEAST

Rosie saw Ma Beacon from a distance as she walked up the path to the old woman's house. Ma Beacon wore a big straw hat as she pruned and cultivated her rose garden in the afternoon sun. Rosie walked slowly yet resolutely, praying all the while. She would now have to face Ma Beacon whose comfort she had surely forsaken for the arms of a desirable and seducing man.

As Rosie slowly approached, Ma Beacon saw her. The minister trotted across the lawn and with a smile that spanned majestically from one ear to the other, welcomed her young compatriot. Rosie reached out to touch Ma Beacon and Ma Beacon grabbed her and held her close.

"I slept with Larry," said Rosie, breathing out a sigh of relief.

. "I know," said Ma Beacon. "I heard. Are you now finished with that relationship?" she asked.

"I am," answered Rosie.

"Do you love him?" asked Ma Beacon.

"He said he would marry me, and I lied to myself and said we were married already. I guess all he wanted was sex, and he lied to me to get it. I was committed to him, I think. I don't like him anymore. I thought I loved him. Now, I don't know.

"Maybe he has feelings for you that he calls love," said Ma Beacon.

"Perhaps he could not bring himself to make the commitment you both need for your relationship to be holy. Love is more than just a feeling. When two people are in love they become one family building one community. Though their individuality remains intact, they become one person."

Ma Beacon clipped a long-stemmed, red rose from the bush and gave it to Rosie, and she beckoned her to an area of the garden where there stood a large, old oak tree.

Under the oak tree a table was set with a pitcher of cool lemonade and two, tall tumblers.

On opposite sides of the table were two reclining lawn chairs. Ma Beacon instructed Rosie to recline on one of the chairs and she handed her a container full of lemonade. Ma Beacon sat back on the other chair. The women looked out over a beautiful lake where ducks and geese swam.

"When a man loves you," continued Ma Beacon, "you will know about it. He will commit himself and his plans to you. There will be no question about his fidelity. He will marry you, because he will want the world to know that you belong to him and that he belongs to you. It means that he loves you enough to build with you in the light where everybody else can see. This does not mean he is a perfect man or that everything he does is right. Your job is to make sure you pick the right one. You do not want to live in a marriage that will destroy you."

Ma Beacon leaned over to Rosie and hushed her voice as though she were whispering and said,

"Jesus loved a woman."

"He did?" said Rosie, in a failed attempt to sound

enthusiastic.

"Yeah, He did," said Ma Beacon slapping Rosie on the thigh.

"Come here, girl," said Ma Beacon reaching out to Rosie. Rosie sat on the soft grass beside the old woman's chair and laid her head on her lap. As Ma Beacon began to stroke Rosie's kinky hair, tears fell down Rosie's cheek and wet Ma Beacon's dress.

"The woman whom Jesus chose to wed was not adorable, though, nor was she a hard-working woman of fortune. She was filthy and ugly in the eyes of many. Some of her teeth were missing. She painted her face to hide putrefying sores erupting from her skin. Her clothes were ragged, and she smelled of bodily waste mixed with the odor of stale incense.

"Surely, no man on earth would want such a woman, but Jesus did. He lived and breathed and gave His all to woo this woman to his side; He wanted to make her his bride."

"Who was this woman," asked Rosie?

"She is you and she is me," answered Ma Beacon.

"She is every woman who has ever suffered the

humiliation of curses laid upon her from generations before. She is every impatient woman who has ever played the fool for the love of strangers instead of waiting on the Lord.

She is every woman who has struggled to maintain her dignity in the face of hate and opposition. And she is not only a woman; she is the church of God."

"But how can you talk about the church of God like that?" asked Rosie. I may not be pure, but the church better be pure," she said desperately.

"Well, you didn't meet Larry in a night club, did you?" asked Ma Beacon.

Rosie grinned nervously at the minister.

"No, I did not," she said.

"We're all sinners," continued Ma Beacon.

"One big difference between many of us and many of the people outside the church is that we know we were created by God and accept the salvation of Jesus Christ.

"The woman whom Jesus loved slept with many men, and because of her infidelity, she became wretched and filthy. In her confusion, she may have reasoned with herself about why she loved strange men, but until she realized Jesus loved her, she was bound in slavery to the devil.

The devil is made rich by our separation from God. He is as a pimp who steals the minds of dejected women who sell their hopes and dreams to him for a moment of intimacy. Jesus had come to claim his bride, and for this He would set her free.

"Ma Beacon," interjected Rosie, "you speak as though Jesus loved a real woman, but you're just talking about the church."

"It's not *just* the church," retorted Ma Beacon.

"Rosie, you are not an afterthought or just another person in the church. You are the thought and meditation of God. He did not die for a group of well-maintained faces attached to a robot body which moves to a "Christian" beat. He died for you. He left the atmosphere of the third heaven which lies beyond the sun, moon and stars, and He entered into the womb of a virgin so He could get close to you."

"But Jesus did not come to marry me," complained Rosie. "He is God. I am a woman. What you are talking about is symbolic."

"That is correct. Jesus is God," admitted Ma Beacon. "If you are to marry and have a family, you must marry a man. But just as the groom and bride figurine on top of the wedding cake is devoid of life, so is the married couple who does not understand the covenant. I am not talking in symbols here. I am revealing the covenant of love to you. It is the essence of marriage. True love is the invisible spirit that binds two people together.

"The first miracle Jesus ever did was at a marriage feast where He turned water into wine. The water that He transformed was poured into six vessels that were used by the Jews for purification. That is what was needed for the church of God, purification. That is what you need, Rosie, purification. We all need to be purified if we want to live a blessed life and love a holy God. Jesus turned the water of purification into wine, and it became the joy of the marriage feast.

"According to the governor of the feast, the wine that Jesus made was the best wine. Jesus' wine was a special wine. According to the prophet Isaiah, it cannot be bought or sold. Read Isaiah 55:1.

"Jesus revealed His passion at the marriage feast. It was the wine given to make the people merry. The wine, the intoxicating, joy-giving drink that Jesus produced from water was given to show the passion and joy of marriage. In the ritual of celebration that took place between the guests and the married couple, joy was inherent, because the wine kept flowing, yea, even the best wine that Jesus made.

"Yet even as the guests of the marriage feast experienced joy, Jesus appeared to be reluctant to perform the miracle. When His mother said, 'They have no wine,' He said to His mother, 'Woman, what have I to do with thee? mine hour is not yet come.' Read John 2:4.

"Upon further investigation, we see that there is no accident that His first miracle was done at a marriage, because the marriage feast signified the essence of His mission to humanity; He had come to marry and to be married. The agony of producing the wine was not yet manifest but its purpose was. The wine is for joy and its true constitution is the blood of Jesus.

"The hour for which Jesus had come was His crucifixion, the passion of Jesus. It was at the crucifixion that He would pay the dowry for the ransom of His bride. In the latter time of Jesus' ministry, the mirth of this beginning of miracles would be turned into sorrow as His mother watched her dear son dying on a rugged cross, blood and water gushing from his wounded side."

"So Jesus came to marry me," said Rosie. "He came to teach me how to love His way; is that what you're saying, Ma Beacon?

"Yes, Rosie," answered Ma Beacon.

"The water represents the desire for love, our willingness to be cleansed so that we may be fit to commune with the Most High in true love," continued the minister.

"The wine is the joy of love provided by the passion of Jesus and transformed into blood at the cross. He laid down His life for you because He wants you to live with Him in eternal communion.

"Jesus' time had not come at the marriage feast. But it did come eventually."

Ma Beacon reached into the pocket of the smock she wore and pulled out a small bottle of rose-scented oil. She daubed some of the oil on the palm of her right hand and applied it to Rosie's forehead. Then she continued speaking.

"The woman whom Christ loves, Rosie, is awakened from her bondage, and she has heard the voice of the man who called her, the Beloved who wooed her. He loves her like none other. He is the Husband who will be in the mind of the good husband.

"He has come to spread His skirt over this, His bride, and He has covered her nakedness and sworn an oath and entered into a covenant with Rosie, and she has become His. (Ezekiel 16:8) Christ has cleansed her so that He can present her to Himself, a 'glorious church, not having spot or wrinkle or any such thing; but that (she) should be Holy and without blemish.'" (Ephesians 5:27)

Ma Beacon removed her hand from Rosie's forehead.

"Stand up, girl," said Ma Beacon.

"Hold your head up, Rosie. You are the one they were trying to be. You are the vessel in which they deposited their jewels."

"Who are *they*, Ma Beacon," asked Rosie.

"I am talking about your mothers. Many of them were cut down as they walked the treacherous highway of this life, but many generations are redeemed in you, Rosie. The ancient faith of your mothers is restored in you."

Rosie stood up and braced herself with the help of a strong woman. As they embraced one another in the warmth of the setting sun, the wind encircled them like the arms of the Spirit.

Rosie walked down the path that led from Ma Beacon's house, and Ma Beacon sat overlooking the lake. The sun was setting now. Reflections of the big orange disk touched the water that rippled with the blowing of the warm breeze. What a mighty painter God is, the sky His canvas, the sun for light.

To some people, Rosie was just as insignificant as one flower plucked from Ma Beacon's garden, but God loved her so much that He condescended to dwell in Rosie's heart. Rosie embraced divinity, and in the arms of God she safely rests.

Statistical data shows that every two minutes, somewhere in America, someone is sexually assaulted.

In 2001, there were 249,000 victims of rape, attempted rape and sexual assault. Because of the methodology of the National Crime Victimization Survey, these figures do not include victims who are 12 or under. Nevertheless, the Justice Department estimates that 1 out of every 6 victims of sexual assault are under the age of 12.

93 percent of juvenile sexual assault victims knew their attacker. 33.3 percent were family members and 58.7 percent were acquaintances.

"One of the most startling aspects of sex crimes is how many go unreported. The most common reasons given by victims for not reporting these crimes are the belief that it is a private or personal matter and that they fear reprisal from the assailant. In 2001 only 38 percent of rapes and sexual assaults were reported to law enforcement officials — about one in every three. Of sexually abused children grades 5 through 12, 41 percent of the boys and 29 percent of the girls had told no one about the abuse — not even a friend or sibling." (See www.rainn.org.)